WHAT ARE WE LIVING FOR?

WHAT ARE WE LIVING FOR?

by

J.G. BENNETT

Title: WHAT ARE WE LIVING FOR?
Author: J.G. Bennett

First published, Hodder & Stoughton, London, October 1949.
This edition published by The J.G. Bennett Foundation

© The Estate of J.G. Bennett & Elizabeth Bennett 2021

Collected Works of J.G. Bennett: Number 2 in the series

wawlf v2: 06162018

CONTENTS

"We have not yet arrived at any reconciliation between history and modern thought—only between half-way history and half-way thought. What the ultimate goal towards which we are moving will be, what this something is which shall bring new life and new regulative principles to coming centuries, we do not know. We can only dimly divine that it will be the mighty deed of some mighty original genius, whose truth and rightness will be proved by the fact that we, working at our poor half thing, will oppose him might and main—we who imagine we long for nothing more eagerly than a genius powerful enough to open up with authority a new path for the world, seeing that we cannot succeed in moving it forward along the track which we have so laboriously prepared."

ALBERT SCHWEITZER
The Quest of the Historical Jesus
(A. & C. Black)

INTRODUCTION

I have written this book with a single definite object—
namely, to show that there is hope that something
seemingly impossible, and yet indispensably necessary
for the future welfare of mankind, can be achieved.
That "something" is the re-establishment of the balance
between the inner and the outer life of man, a balance
that has been destroyed by many causes but chiefly
through the mistakes of so-called Western Civilization.
References to the disparity between man's power to
act upon the external world and his ability to control
himself have been made so often that they have become
trite and even boring. The truism, so often uttered after
each of the recent world wars, that it is dangerous to
put a loaded weapon in the hands of a child has now
ceased to attract attention. The world has put aside
thoughts of its own childishness and is busily engaged
in forging weapons which even a wise man would not
dare to possess. And yet no one denies the truth of the
basic judgment that, in the ordering of human relationships, we have made no progress corresponding to the
advances made in our powers of hurting ourselves and
of destroying one another's existence.

Another truism which reflects the age-long experience of mankind is that no organization can work better

than can the people who compose it. Ancient experience and recent experience equally must convince us that the ordering of human affairs cannot be achieved by any organization the working of which depends on people who themselves are slaves of egoism, vanity, ambition, the desire for power, suspicion distrust, partiality, prejudice and all the other forces which we see operating in every group of human beings throughout the world without distinction of nation, race or creed. The apparent hopelessness of the situation lies precisely in this, that whereas we are capable of devising any kind of mechanism, we are incapable of making a free impartial being, capable of rational behaviour—that is, a *man*. No form of exhortation, no promises and no threats can arouse people to rational behaviour unless they are inwardly free. This should be obvious; but no one takes so simple a fact into account. And so we find book after book written, sermon after sermon preached, one political declaration after another made, all stopping short of the one crucial step—namely, at the point at which it becomes necessary to explain how human nature can be changed.

It would not be fair to say that no attempts are made to go beyond this point, but it is necessary to see what the attempts made amount to and where they can be expected to lead. The first can be described as religious optimism. It is based upon the conviction that there is in the teaching and practice of one or another religious institution such power that it is only

necessary to bring men and women in closer contact
with this power, for it to operate and bring about
the needed change. If this were true, this book need
not have been written. But what are the inescapable
facts? Islam has existed for 1200 years, Christianity for nearly 2000 and Buddhism for nearly 2500.
Judaism is even more ancient. The teaching of all
religions concerning the importance of man's inner
life is almost identical. In each of them institutions
of various kinds have been formed to strengthen and
systematize their message to the world. There is no
indication whatever that as time has passed men have
become better Christians, more devout Moslems, more
faithful to the teachings of Gotama or Moses. Within
each of these religious communities great saints have
arisen from time to time to lead short-lived revivals
of faith and the practice of religion. There have been
periods when saints were recognized as such even in
their lifetime, but we must ask ourselves in all serious-
ness what chance a true saint would have today in any
of the religious communities of the world. Bearing in
mind not merely the decay of religious faith but also
the presence of powerful forces, forces not so much
actively hostile to, as contemptuous of, religion (for
there is not even the stimulus of religious persecution), we are forced to the conclusion that religious
optimism of the kind which assumes that the religious
forces already operating in the world are sufficient to
bring about a change in human life, is unfounded and
delusive. Religious optimism breaks down precisely at

the point where it becomes necessary to show how
people are to be made to live and act as their religion
teaches.

The Founder of Christianity, speaking "as one having
authority, and not as the scribes," made a prophecy the
full tragic import of which is becoming clear only after
2000 years, when he said: "Everyone that heareth
these sayings of mine, and doeth them not, shall be
likened unto a foolish man, which built his house upon
the sand. And the rain descended, and the floods came,
and the winds blew, and beat upon that house; and it
fell, and great was the fall of it." Christians have done
many remarkable things, but, in their doings, they have
not done according to the words of Christ: the house of
Christianity has fallen, and cannot be rebuilt. The same
is true of Islam, although, perhaps by reason of a less
austere demand upon the frailty of human nature, the
precepts of Mohammed are still observed more honestly
than is the teaching of Christ. This was impressed on
me when last year I visited Omdurman, one of the few
cities of the world entirely inhabited by Moslems, and
witnessed the simple fervour with which the whole
city stopped its work to observe the evening ritual
prayer. Unfortunately, in most parts of the world the
very name, Moslem, has come to bear a political rather
than a religious meaning. The same, alas, is true of the
religion of Moses and the Hebrew Prophets. Again,
there was once a time when to be called a Hindu was an
indication that a man had religious faith, was resistant

to forcible conversion to the religion of an invader and accepted the persecution which this resistance incurred. Even when a man, in many respects a true saint, emerged to lead a Hindu revival, he could not liberate himself from the political implications of religious conflict. Buddhism, which claims more adherents than any other religious system in the world, has fulfilled only too surely the prophecy of its Founder, that within five hundred years his followers would have split up into mutually opposing sects and in a thousand years would have lost the very heart of his teaching. "Everyone that heareth these sayings of mine, and doeth them not," rings out as an accusation addressed without distinction to the followers of all the religious systems of the world.

The reaction against religion has taken the form of abandoning the belief that anything can be done—or even needs to be done—about the inner life of man, and placing reliance upon external organization. Humanitarianism is the acceptance, explicit or implicit, of man as he is; with the corollary that with this "man as he is" the task must be undertaken of securing human welfare. In some of its manifestations, from the *contrat social* to the benevolent mother state, humanitarianism is based on the assumption that men are naturally good and, if not spoiled by wrong forms of external organization, are capable of living happy and fruitful lives in harmony with one another. Another manifestation of humanitarianism takes a more cynical view of human nature, regarding the masses as helpless—even perhaps hopeless—and therefore in need of authoritative direction from an enlightened few. In both cases there is one fundamental postulate—namely, that those responsible for the working of whatever organization may be involved are capable of wise and disinterested action: a postulate contradicted by the unequivocal evidence of history and by all our present experience. I wrote that all proposals for bettering the situation of mankind stop short at the point where it becomes necessary to explain how people themselves are to be changed: humanitarianism proceeds by the ridiculous expedient of ignoring the central problem and hoping for the best.

"Hoping for the best" is one symptom of a disease from which mankind has always suffered: the inability to face facts. This disease has always been endemic in mankind but perhaps never more dangerously so than at the present time. One peculiar con-sequence of the disease is that, when it is imperatively necessary to do one thing which may be difficult or disagreeable, people at once occupy themselves with doing something quite different and shut their eyes to the fact that the real problem remains unsolved. The nature, the cause and the possible cure of the disease constitute one of the principal themes of this book.

Philosophers, priests, serious and would-be serious writers, and even politicians, have been saying that the advance in our power "to control nature" (as they say), must be accompanied by a corresponding change in the

ability of people to live and work in harmony together.
It is often, and rightly, observed that the problem has
grown more difficult with the development of methods
of communication which have made the world smaller
and brought nations and races in closer contact than at
any previous period of recorded history. The problem is
accentuated by the division of labour without which no
modern economic system could exist. It is made urgent
by the invention and elaboration of terrible weapons of
destruction. It is made obvious by the growing suspicion
and misunderstanding between the peoples of the world.
And yet nothing is done even to attempt a solution of
the central problem. World organizations are set up to
study every imaginable problem of health, education
and social welfare, the production and distribution
of primary materials and manufactured commodities,
political organization and the means of avoiding war.
But no world organization exists to study the problem
of human nature itself, and to ascertain whether and by
what means there can be secured the harmonious development of man from his present enslavement to his own
egoism and all the consequences of it, to that state of
inward freedom, impartiality and wisdom which alone
would entitle him to the proud name of Man.

Recently, a group of engineers and scientists in
London initiated an enquiry into the question: "Can
Psychology help to prevent war?" Representatives
of various schools of psychological thought, and
also several organizations founded for some purpose

such as the promotion of international goodwill, took part in the enquiry. I was allowed to see an analysis of the replies and found, as I had expected, that almost all were concerned with influencing other people but scarcely one even considered the central problem of changing the inner being of the individual himself.

I am well aware, of course, that educationalists conceive their mission in terms of preparing the next generation for a more normal and harmonious existence than that of their parents. Many educationalists— probably the great majority—would assert that their task is at least as much concerned with questions of "character" as with teaching the various kinds of skill required for assuring a comfortable material existence. Nevertheless, as I endeavour to show in the chapter on Education, this preoccupation with questions of character is entirely devoid of any practical outcome; nor is there any serious attempt to understand what kind of work is required on the part of the teacher or on the part of the pupil if any concrete results are to be achieved. Indeed, the educational systems in vogue in most countries today are even more pernicious than were those of the past in respect of implanting foolish ideas alongside a complete absence of the capacity for impartial judgment.

If we ask ourselves how it is possible, that the very sensible diagnosis of our troubles in terms of the disparity between our inner and our outer powers does not lead to any effective action, we find a two-fold

answer. First, no one even begins to attempt to find any
way in which the inner life of man could be changed
within a period of time sufficiently short to enable the
impending disaster to be averted. This failure, as I have
said, results in "hoping for the best." Secondly, there
exists a state which might be described almost equally
well as weak optimism or weak pessimism. It consists
in throwing forward into the distant future the prospect
of better things. Thus, there are people who say that,
sooner or later, mankind is bound to learn from a series
of disasters that it is impossible to live at all on the
basis of an unrestrained egoism. After the next war, or
the next war but one, or the nth war, they say, we shall
at last have learned that the fire of egoism burns, and
then there will emerge a new kind of humanity possessing what is called "world consciousness" and therefore
able to accept and live by some kind of world government. All such hopes, for what they are worth, shatter
on the rock of experience. Mankind has never learned
to profit by any lesson, however bitter, and it is at least
as probable that a series of destructive wars, terminated
only by exhaustion, will lead to the complete degeneration of the human race, as that there will emerge a
hitherto undisclosed capacity for world-wide coopera-
tion. It is a fundamental principle that everything good
comes only as a result of conscious effort and never
from the action of accidental blind forces.

Inexorably we are brought back to the starting
point that human nature must be changed, and that the

striving for this must take precedence over all other
labours however important and urgent these may
appear to be. There is no other way out. The progress
of science and technology cannot be stopped. The
interpenetration of economic and social systems, the
impact of race upon race and of nation upon nation
will continue and increase in intensity. The complexity
of life will grow with a corresponding growth in the
demand upon men and women for mutual tolerance and
understanding. This demand cannot be met by men and
women such as we are today and shall remain unless
the task of bringing about at least an indispensable
minimal diminution of egoism and its consequences is
undertaken and accomplished.

So far I have said nothing that has not been said
better and more forcibly many times before. We
still remain at the threshold with the question of
Nicodemus. Before attempting an answer which
will apply to the present condition of our world, it
behooves me to make one distinction without which
the whole meaning of what I have already stated is lost.
We must distinguish between real change and fictitious change. The change which comes from without,
from externally imposed training and discipline, is
fictitious. Man is a highly suggestible animal and is
able to respond to a remarkable degree to reiterated
impressions received from without. His reflexes can
be conditioned. Behaviour patterns can be and are
imposed on him by his education, by the conventions
current in his environment, and by the multiform fears

which surround his life. At the present time, all these factors operate upon the human psyche almost exclusively as poisons. Even if they could be changed so as no longer to produce specifically harmful effects man would still remain as he is now, an unconscious slave of his own egoism. He still would have no defense against the disruptive tendencies which arise automatically among beings whose desires outstrip their means of satisfaction. It is in this sense that modifications produced in the behaviour pattern by external influences must be called fictitious changes only.

Real change comes from within, by conscious work intentionally performed by the being himself. Only from such conscious work can come the inward freedom and impartiality necessary for harmonious existence. To many people the distinction I have made will be by no means self-evident. Indeed, it is the first stumbling block on the way to discovering the means to be employed for securing the future welfare of mankind. Even those who have realized the impossibility of achieving by external organization alone, a better life for the many, very often transfer their hope to the effects of the process of education and training on the individual. It is not necessary to argue in detail the futility of such a hope, because it depends upon an external change in the organization of human affairs, and the possibility of change is ruled out if we admit that no organization can work for good unless those who compose it are, at least to some degree, already liberated from egoism. All the degenerative factors of vanity, self-will, prejudice, suspicion and the rest, are already present in those responsible for devising and carrying out educational systems. Everything that pours from a poisoned vessel must itself be tainted. The history of education teaches us that every kind of means has been tried for "improving" people through influences external to themselves, and that all have failed; not least those which are used in different countries at the present day.

All this only serves to bring into relief the difficulty of our task. If mankind is to be saved man himself must change; but he does not know how to change and, most terrifying of all, he does not particularly want to. He does not even know what change means. He may dimly realize that something could be achieved by particularly difficult efforts running counter equally to his formed habits and his inner impulses. If he be a Christian, for example, he may dimly perceive that to live in fact and without compromise according to the injunctions of the Sermon on the Mount, would turn upside down not only his life but also his very nature. And, recognizing that if he were to follow that path nothing at all would remain of the life to which he is accustomed, he turns aside to some other way of life more in keeping with what he conceives to be his powers and his needs. Contemplating the Sermon on the Mount, I return to the phrase I used at the beginning of this Introduction to describe the seemingly impossible and yet indispensably necessary something for which we are seeking. We may start by consoling

ourselves with the thought that the seeming impossibility of finding the "something" may be the very
reason why the way is not obvious to everyone. Wolfe
conquered Quebec because the French left undefend-
ed the cliff which it was deemed impossible to scale.
Assuming, without serious investigation, that human
nature is a datum of stubborn fact that must be taken
unchanged into any plan of action, the reformers have
been driven to search for a way out along the seemingly
hopeful but actually closed path of social organization.

So far so good—or so bad. We are to seek for means
of achieving a seemingly impossible change in human
nature. But what is this change to be? The inner life of
men has not been without its share of attention from
those who are concerned over the state of man. The
term, perennial philosophy, first used by Leibnitz in
quite another connection, has recently come into vogue
to describe the age-old belief that true welfare is the
welfare of the spirit. This belief is associated in varying
degrees with the idealistic philosophy which asserts
that reality belongs to experience and not to things. It
very often leads to some form of Quietism or withdraw-
al from the outer world into an inner world where peace
and security are alone to be found. It sees suffering
as an evil to be escaped from or at best as a means
through which liberation can be attained. It pities, but
does not plunge into, the distressed world. Much that
goes under the name of mysticism belongs to this kind
of preoccupation with the inner life. In recent times

the word, mysticism, has become almost a term of reproach, generally used in opposition to sound or robust commonsense. It is regarded as being tainted with an unscientific disregard for facts. All this is rather strange in view of the subjectivist trend of the philosophy of science at the present time. Many eminent scientists whose orthodox standing is beyond dispute have given utterance to views on the nature of reality and the kind of ultimate explanation underlying the scientific conception of the world, which could be translated almost word for word into the language of oriental mysticism.

But all this is of no real importance, since these discussions have no bearing upon the problem of changing human nature. I am concerned only to characterize a group of views differing widely in points of detail but agreeing in principle that the subjective experience is what ultimately matters. It is true that a Christian mystic like Meister Eckhart could say: "If a man were in ecstasy and rapt up to the fifth heaven and were to see his even Christian in want of a loaf of bread, I would say it would be his duty to leave his ecstasy and provide for that man's Need." It is clear, however, that in saying this Eckhart conceives the mystic as making a sacrifice of his own welfare in performing the act of charity. In this lies the crux of the distinction which I am concerned here to make. There is pre-occupation with the inner life for its own sake, and there is concern over the inner life because its defects mar the outer life. There is the distinction between being for being's sake, and being for the sake of doing. Strangely enough this distinction is very seldom made, and its importance hardly ever recognized, by those who concern themselves with these questions. But it is vital for our present theme. It is no solution—or at best but a poor solution—to the problem of a suffering world to suggest that as many people as possible should find a way of escape from it.

The way is now open for a more specific statement of what I mean by the change in human nature. I have excluded two kinds of change, both of which are, in fact, possible. The first is the fictitious change brought about by external agencies without the conscious labour of the individual concerned: this can be called external change for an external objective. The second false change is that which leads to internal change without external objective. There is no doubt that by appropriate methods mystical experiences can be realized and that these experiences are of supreme importance and value to the person concerned. They can be reached without effort by the use of drugs or as a result of particular pathological conditions of the physical organism. They can be reached to a limited degree by way of certain kinds of special exercise, such as those to be found in manuals of Christian Mysticism or those which go by the name of Yoga. They can be reached to a very high degree by the practice of austerity which demands from the individual complete renunciation of all other aims in life and usually involves his retirement into a Monastery or Yogi school. Much can be learned about them by an attentive study of the lives, and especially the autobiographies and writings, of saints and mystics. Mystical experiences are by no means always incompatible with a useful external life; in most cases those who have attained them accept as a duty the endeavour to admit a group of immediate disciples to as large a share in the experiences as they are able to assimilate. But in so far as the experience is made the primary objective and the external work is regarded as only secondary in importance, such practices belong to the category of the inner life for the sake of the inner life, or being for the sake of being. There is no doubt that mysticism of this kind has played a large part in the rise and development of religious institutions; as has been made clear, for example, by Von Hegel and Dean Inge. In the formulation of religious dogma, the orthodox theologian of every religion has drawn, often to a greater extent than he would be prepared to admit, upon the data of mystical experience. I am not concerned primarily, or even to an important extent, with this aspect of the inner life. For one thing, history teaches us that mysticism of the purely subjective kind has been unable to make any great contribution towards bettering the life of man.

Preoccupation with bodily necessities, with human relationships and with anxiety about the future dominates the life of the average man and woman. Into this preoccupation enters the poison of egoism with all its attendant miseries. These are the things with which we must be concerned if we are moved by compassion for the suffering of the world. It is because these things are so inextricably woven into the very fabric of human nature as we know it that the inner and the outer life cannot be separated or the welfare of one pursued to the exclusion of the other. It is not a question of finding how the inner life of man can so be changed that he is himself liberated from suffering, but how it can be changed so that he can live a becoming outer life.

This, admittedly, is an over-simplification of the problem. I have not, for example, referred to death. We are mortal, and the question must arise whether our destiny is to be conceived only in terms of this life that we know or in terms of some actual or possible existence beyond the grave. In speaking of the suffering of the world I have not referred to the belief formerly very widely and strongly held, but now probably absent or very weak among most people, that the suffering and failure of this visible life are compensated in another life which is somehow assured without any special or extraordinary efforts on the part of the being concerned. I shall not say much about this for the reason, among others, that, objectively understood, life and death are not separate and the task of living a becoming life is identical with that of dying a becoming death. If egoism is a taint in life, it is as certainly a source of terror in the face of death; for who can doubt that if any further existence is open to man, in it the fruits of egoism will be very bitter.

I have used the word, egoism, as a compendious description of all those factors which poison human relationships and which it is "seemingly impossible" to eradicate.

Every practical objective requires for its attainment a sequence of coordinated actions. In the absence of prior knowledge, the only method available is that which is known as "hit or miss," or "trial and error"— the method which enables the captive rat finally to thread his way through the labyrinth. When the problem exceeds a certain complexity—more exactly, when the time available is shorter than the time required to find the solution—it cannot be solved by this means. The experience of many thousands of years has shown that this method is useless when applied to the betterment of man. It is hardly possible for a man to discover for himself and put into practice within the short span of his effective life, the means of changing his own being. And the time available is really shorter than this, for it is necessary first, that a man come to the realization that a change is needed and secondly, when he has brought about the change in himself, that he have time to use it for the good of others. Knowledge, therefore, is necessary—knowledge which can be obtained only from those who already possess it—of what must be done and how to do it. For there must be a technique of inner work just as there is a technique of outer work. The difference is that men throughout the world occupy themselves with the development of external techniques, not suspecting that it is even more important to discover the technique of changing oneself. Were it the case that this technique had yet to be discovered our situation would indeed be serious, for the reason that there is barely a hope of finding it unaided in a single lifetime. Realization of this has led some to seek for the required knowledge in places where according to rumor it has been found and preserved over long periods of time. The traditional "Wisdom of the East" refers precisely to this technique of inner work, but there are differences so great as to divide this wisdom into categories which have scarcely anything in common one with another. There is the traditional wisdom concerned with subjective experience only, to which I have already referred. Access to this is by no means difficult for anyone who seeks it with resolution and is prepared to persist, perhaps for many years, until he discovers an authentic source. Those who regard high mystical experience— such as the Samadhi of the Yogis—as the summit of human attainment, do not look beyond the sources of knowledge of this first kind. Since these are the people who chiefly have written about the Wisdom of the East, the belief has grown up that there is nothing to be found but these subjective techniques. There is, however, a deeper and less accessible tradition of schools which possess knowledge of a high order concerned with "being for the sake of doing." Closely associated with this is the legend which recurs openly in the mythologies and secretly in certain records, of a Golden Age when these

methods of achieving being for the sake of doing were
widely known and practiced and when, in consequence,
the exterior life of man attained for a period a degree of
harmony and wellbeing which has never since been known.
Archaeological research has taught us to respect such
traditions, for it almost invariably happens that when a
means is found for verifying them their historical value
becomes apparent.

So long as the "Wisdom of the East" is conceived
only in terms of mysticism and a certain contempt for
the problems and sufferings of the world, no very great
importance attaches to the investigation of its sources.
But everything acquires a new colour in the light of
the suggestion that the East may have possessed
knowledge of techniques for the development of being
for the sake of doing. The knowledge of the external
world and the power to control external things has
been gained in the West in a very short space of time
by the work of many thousands of trained research
workers. May it not be possible that discoveries of
not less importance concerning the inner life of man
have been made in the East by small groups of workers
communicating their results from generation to generation over thousands of years? It is even possible
to suggest why there should be such a difference in
the two processes. Knowledge of the external world,
and particularly knowledge obtainable by scientific
research, is of such a character that it can be adequately
expressed and transmitted in words. It can, therefore,

without particular difficulty, be shared and used by
very large numbers of people. Knowledge of man's
inner nature, and especially knowledge relating to the
techniques whereby that inner nature can be changed,
is almost impossible to describe in words and can be
transmitted only by the combined personal efforts of
teacher and pupil. Such knowledge can be preserved
over very long periods of time, but it cannot readily
be disseminated and made widely available to those
who need it. If we can be convinced, however, that
such knowledge must exist, we have at least a hopeful
starting-point for further research. I remember discussing this nearly thirty years ago with that remarkable
man, the late PETER DAMIAN OUSPENSKY. He had made
it his life's work to verify for himself whether or not
there really existed schools of practical teaching as
distinct from schools concerned only with subjective experience. He had reached the conclusion that
unless such knowledge existed and could be found
there was no hope of liberating people from their
growing slavery to a mechanized existence. This
being so, the search for such knowledge—however
slender the hope that it might be found—assumed an
importance far greater than any other line of investigation and study—however hopeful that line might
appear. In his book, *A New Model of the Universe*,
Ouspensky gave some indication of the evidence which
had convinced him that real knowledge of the kind I
have been discussing does in fact exist. He promised
to give in a later book, *Fragments of an Unknown*

Teaching,* an account of the teaching he had found. Twenty-one years have passed since that day, and now at last it has been made known that the promised volume will be published soon.

To most people who have interested themselves in these matters it is no secret that the teaching to which Ouspensky referred is that of GEORGE GURDJIEFF. Those of us who during the past thirty years have had the advantage of "supping at his ideas table," are satisfied that in him we have found in the fullest measure just that knowledge—above all of practical methods of work—which is needed before one can embark with real hope of success upon the task of creating one's own being.

The approach to Gurdjieff's ideas is very difficult for anyone who comes with preconceived ideas about the form which a valid teaching should take. Everything and everyone is turned upside down. Naturally, it is hard to agree to be turned upside down when one is convinced that one is already the right way up.

The present book may help those who are interested in the prospect of a wider dissemination of Gurdjieff's teaching, to discern for themselves that nearly all our current views and beliefs about man and his world are topsy-turvy.

---

* [Later published as *In Search of the Miraculous.* Ed.]

CHAPTER I

MAN—THINKING ANIMAL OR
REASONABLE BEING

K NOWLEDGE and Wisdom are commonly contrast-
ed in their significance for the life of man. The
distinction can be misleading, but it will serve as a
starting-point for a discussion of the human situation.
There are certain objectives which can be attained
through knowledge; others require wisdom. Mankind
has been remarkably successful in the former and even
more remarkably unsuccessful in the latter. Unfortunately, the wellbeing of man depends upon the
attainment of objectives of the second kind. It is not
knowledge, but wisdom, that determines whether a
man can be at peace with himself, can live in harmony
with his immediate environment, can send his children
into the world rightly prepared for their task in life,
can judge and discriminate between the many external
influences which constantly move him to action. It
is wisdom, and not knowledge, that determines the
success or failure of all organized human activities,
especially those which are directed to lofty aims, such
as the right ordering of human existence, the establish-
ment of harmonious relationships between groups of
people and the prevention of war. In all these things
the record of history is one of reiterated failure; and

today we see failure all around us. Moreover, the greater the scale of operation the greater the probability of failure. We do find—though too seldom—individuals relatively free in themselves and living contented lives in harmony with their neighbours. We find—though even more seldom—families in which a true harmony prevails and a consistent thread of purpose and understanding runs through the years of common family experience. But when we turn to larger organizations and greater purposes we find only the most evanescent traces of wisdom in the deliberations and actions of these bodies, for all their high-sounding names.

The things that men want most, these they cannot achieve. There are also, of course, many things which they cannot do and do not want to do. One of these is to face facts and draw honest conclusions from them. The facts are quite clear. We do not achieve our purposes; and especially is this the case when those purposes are of such a nature that they require wise judgment and disinterested action. The better our intentions and the nobler our motives the more certain it is that we shall fail to accomplish the tasks to which we set our hand. When we look at the good accomplishments of mankind we can see that almost invariably they are initiated by some individual or group of people with "good" intentions who fail to carry them to a conclusion. At a certain point various factors begin to operate: ambition in one, desire for power in another, vanity, obstinacy or distrust in a third; from the operation of these factors the process goes forward but it invariably departs in some essential way from the conception which lay at its origin. When the results are on a sufficiently large scale they are labelled "good" without it being taken into account whether or not they really conduce to the welfare of mankind or of that community or group in which they are experienced.

And as we have an inveterate habit of accepting this labelling we evade the task of enquiring whether these "good" results correspond at all to the original intentions or whether, in any objective sense, they are good at all.

Let us, take as a characteristic example, known to all, the history of universal suffrage. The 18th-century reformers who proclaimed this as an ideal, conceived it as the means of assuring that every man and woman of responsible age would have an equal and effective voice in determining the legislation under which they would be governed. One immediate outcome was the French Revolution and the Napoleonic Wars, events surely as remote as is possible from the purposes of the reformers. Universal male suffrage was written into the American Constitution, but the operation of the two-party system has been such that the individual voter is confronted with a situation in which he usually is obliged to choose between alternatives neither of which corresponds to his own wishes: he votes, in fact, not in favour of this or that legislative programme but according either to a habit implanted in him from childhood or in response to some emotional impulse of like or dislike, an impulse more often than not attached to some person who happens to be the figurehead of one or another party.

In the British self-governing territories universal suffrage has in the past operated in much the same way. In other countries, where many political parties exist, the voter apparently has a greater opportunity of exercising his choice in accordance with a detailed analysis of his wishes. In practice, however, the situation works out even more unfavourably, and the many party system provides one of the outstanding examples of unwisdom in the conduct of human affairs. Petty personal motives, ambition, the desire for power and even for material gain are virtually the sole factors which determine the grouping of parties; never in any single case the desires and intentions of the Voters by whom the members were elected. I am not concerned here with the *reductio ad absurdum* of universal suffrage seen in the one-party system, in which elections serve merely as a vehicle for propaganda to strengthen the position of the group controlling the destinies of the State. The really significant lesson is the one which is to be learned from those countries where universal suffrage still does operate in such a way as to make the individual voter an important factor in political calculations. Being unversed in the complicated problems of political economy and international affairs, the voter cannot come to an independent decision which would make his own personal views really effective. So it becomes necessary to present him with a simplified statement, and the task of preparing these statements is in the hands of the political parties which seek his suffrage. Were these parties able to display wisdom and courage in presenting statements which, though simplified, would nevertheless correspond to the knowledge of the facts which they, with their wider sources of information, should possess, the voter might be able to make a choice which at least would have some relation to the reality of the situation. In practice exactly the opposite occurs: every effort is made to disguise the reality of the situation; elections take place in a fictitious atmosphere and are decided in terms of factors such as personal likes and dislikes directed towards or against the party leaders, or promises which those who make them know—or should know—they will be unable to fulfil. So the wheel turns full circle. The original purpose, which was to place the individual voter in effectual control over the legislation under which he will be governed, has now been lost and a situation has arisen in which executives are in full control; but these, in order to maintain themselves in power, are obliged to direct propaganda towards the individual voter, with the intention of influencing his personal judgment and depriving him of effective power of choice. The individual voter cannot decide whom he will vote for, or what he will vote for; seldom does he even understand the issues involved.

Most people can succeed in not taking seriously

such failures of purpose as that which I have just described, but there is one situation towards which it is scarcely possible to be indifferent. This is the failure of mankind to prevent war. Gurdjieff terms war "the periodic process of the reciprocal destruction of one another's existence." The description. is important because it puts into its true perspective the horror of this terrible phenomenon. Only a mind bordering on the pathological can regard war as anything but a shameful stain on the human race. Under more or less normal conditions—that is, in the absence of the peculiar mass psychosis which occurs at the onset of war—the overwhelming majority of all peoples regard the possibility of war with repugnance and dread. And yet, not only do wars occur, but in recent times they have also assumed a new and particularly shameful character: (they now involve, not only the ruthless slaughter of opposing armies with inhuman weapons, but even the indiscriminate destruction of defenceless women and children, with continuing consequences that may reach the lives of generations yet unborn.

It goes without saying that unbecoming characteristics of the human psyche such as the desire for power, selfishness, laziness and all forms of unwisdom, are operative in rendering the peoples defenceless against the onset of war psychosis. There is, however, something deeper and hitherto unexplained in the psychosis itself. The same people who a few years previously viewed with horror and dismay the remotest possibility of mass destruction of others' existence, become victims of that most peculiar psychic condition in which the shame of an act of mutual destruction is replaced by a quite definite desire to destroy: they become convinced that destruction is justified. The conviction very often has its beginning in a process of mental justification: self-defense, for example, or the need to liberate some other people from an oppressor; but the formula itself is soon forgotten and the desire for destruction is all that remains until the peculiar psychosis passes and people revert to what surely is the more normal state of natural horror at the process of destruction.

How does this all come about? How is it that the human race from time to time is unable to resist the tendency to fall into a psychic state which reason and heart alike condemn? How is it that we are able neither ourselves to avoid., nor to join with others in preventing, the things that from the bottom of our hearts we know are against our own common interest?

The only satisfactory explanation of which I am aware is given by Gurdjieff in terms of two independently operating factors; but before I discuss it, I must say something about one conception which has dominated human thought for nearly 2500 years and which originated, so far as the Western world is concerned, in the theories of the Greek philosophers about man, his nature and his place in the universe. This is the conception of Reason, identified with the operation of the human brain. The underlying assumption is, that if a man is able to think clearly and

see what is either subjectively desirable or objectively proper, he will regulate his life accordingly and
so gradually liberate himself from subjection to the
unreasoning animal impulses responsible for his sufferings and failures. The belief in Reason has undergone
vicissitudes as various ways of applying the principle
have been tried and found wanting. The last wave of
optimism began in the 17th century, and if its origin
can be associated with any one name it must surely be
that of Descartes, whose doctrine was the supremacy of
the human mind. In the 18th century, Reason—always
identified with the automatic processes of the cerebral
hemispheres of the human central nervous system—
was enthroned as the Power which should lead mankind
to a humanitarian millennium. Greek thought having
already triumphed over Christian tradition in the age of
Scholasticism, the churches were defenceless against
these essentially anti-religious conceptions. The
doctrine that to think rightly was to act rightly became
almost an axiom, and forgotten were the words of Saint
Paul: "For that which I do I allow not: for what I would,
that do I not; but what I hate, that do I."

Until the present century the belief prevailed—and
indeed for many people it prevails today—that the
human mind was capable of finding a solution to human
problems and piloting us into some safe harbour where
we should be able to live a more normal existence
than that of our forefathers. These hopes have, with
extraordinary rapidity, started to fade. Instead of

giving place to a determination to find out why, and, at whatever cost, to discover a more reliable way, hope has given place to a general apathy and a most prevalent desire at all costs to avoid thinking. Such processes go by waves, and it happens that at this very moment as I write, we are passing through a state, common to the whole world, of being dominated by the desire not to think about things as they really are. During the last year I have had occasion to visit many countries in three continents. I have just returned from my second recent visit to the United States. Wherever I have gone I have been impressed by the prevalence of the disease of "hoping for the best". Immediately after the Second World War a very disturbed state of mind was to be sensed everywhere a feeling of threat to the future of the human race arising from the development of our technical powers without a corresponding advance in our ability to regulate our lives. Conditions have not changed, but people now accept the flimsiest excuse for hoping for the best. It is enough for some Professor to say that such and such a kind of bomb is not going to be so bad after all for people at once to put out of their minds the thought of the horror of war and trust themselves to their favourite process of grasping for immediate petty satisfactions. Or, should a famous economist declare that the economic situation is improving, people cease to concern themselves over the extraordinary breakdown in the efficiency of the productive mechanism of the world. We may be sure that the present period of unreasoning optimism will pass and a new phase of alarm and tension set in and that a time will come when the tension will be so acute that it is very difficult to see what can prevent a fresh conflagration. And this brings me back to the subject of war and its causes.

It is usual to ascribe the cause of war to human intentions and to conceive war as a conflict between good and bad intentions. The term, aggressor, has become a convenient label with which to impute evil intentions to one group and, by inference, good intentions to another. It goes without saying that this applies equally to both sides in any conflict, so that war always appears to all those who take part in it as being undertaken in defense of some sacred principle or to promote some worthy cause. Now, the passionate conviction that it is necessary and right, and even a sacred duty, to destroy the existence of other beings, is precisely the psychosis which we must seek to understand. This we cannot hope to do unless, we place ourselves in an objective and impartial position. A study of history should teach us, but it is difficult to learn its lessons because historical books invariably are written from a subjective and partial standpoint by authors who, despite professed intentions to the contrary, identify themselves with some particular point of view. When we do recognise the indubitable fact that wars do not arise from evil intentions we are forced to realize that they imply a peculiar universal helplessness which goes deeper than the ordinary failures of our daily lives. When war comes, the people who hated the very thought of it are seized with the desire to destroy, and so long as they have confidence in their own weapons and believe in the possibility of winning, they continue to work for destruction. In the mildest and most humane people pity dries up, and without any sense of shame they enjoy accounts of the destruction of cities and the slaughter of women and children.

As I said before, the explanation of war given by Gurdjieff in his teaching is that it arises from two quite independent factors. The first is the appearance of a state of tension which is not due to human agencies, and the second is the reaction of people to such tension.' The state of tension arises from general processes of a planetary nature involving the equilibrium of the process of transformation of energy in the solar system as a whole. This state of tension induces in people a general dissatisfaction with things as they are. Such dissatisfaction is not in itself a bad thing nor is there any necessity for it to lead to any process of destruction. On the contrary it should, if people were capable of a normal response—that is, if there were present in them a feeling of need for self-perfection—cause them to react to such periods of tension by greater efforts to bring about in themselves that change of being which is necessary for their ultimate welfare. But in the absence of any understanding of this need for inward change, the pressure is transferred into their external relationships and operates upon those psychic factors of egoism, desire for power, suspicion, jealousy and the rest, which in turn develop by contagion into the mass psychosis which makes war possible. I shall revert to this later when I have explained in a little more detail some of the fundamental principles of Gurdjieff's system.

If we are to arrive at any understanding of the human problem, we must first try to answer the question: What is man himself? Is he a machine, enmeshed without the possibility of free movement in the causal mechanism of the physical world? Is he an animal like any other animal, eating and being eaten, reproducing his kind and perishing utterly when his body dies? Or is he, not just an ordinary animal, but something different on account of his conscious experience and power of choice? Is he a special creation made in the image of God, an infinitely precious immortal soul? Different people give different answers to these seemingly incompatible questions. One man will maintain, even with passion, that man is only a machine. Another will insist that he is an immortal soul. This is not very strange, for people always hold the strongest convictions about the things which they do not understand. What is, however, very strange and scarcely credible is that in most cases there would be no difference in the behaviour of the two men holding these opposite views. An immortal soul is surely the most valuable treasure which a being could possess, and yet those who claim that they have one very seldom concern themselves seriously with its welfare. To assert that man is a machine is surely to make all life indifferent and meaningless, and yet those who do so are as full of passions and strivings as if they were convinced that they were free and independent beings. The fact was brought home to pie some years ago when an eminent biologist, noted for his unswerving adherence to a mechanistic doctrine, announced triumphantly in my presence that after years of striving he had succeeded in forcing the British Broadcasting Corporation to accept a broadcast from the standpoint of atheistic mechanism! The reason for these inconsistencies is that convincing arguments can be found for any of the implied conceptions of human nature, and the man who by temperament or some accident of his early education adheres, to any one, cannot wholly divest himself of the others.

All these vehement assertions about human nature mask an underlying state of bewildered ignorance. Nothing makes sense. If we are machines, why do we feel so strongly the reality of our power of choice? If we have an immortal soul, why can we find no evidence of its existence? If we are free beings, why do we behave like slaves? If we are animals, why do we speculate about our destiny? I have not, encountered any more convincing explanation of these contradictions than that which is given by Gurdjieff. It is very simple. The confusion arises because we fail to distinguish between what man is and what he might be. According to Gurdjieff, man does not possess a pre-existent immortal soul; but in the course of his life a soul becomes formed to a greater or lesser degree of perfection according to the way in which his life is lived. The soul of map is not the cause, but the consequence, of his behaviour. He is not free in the sense of being exempt from the causal mechanism of the world; but he has a limited power of choice. When he does not exercise this power of choice he is a machine and his activity, like that of other machines, is determined solely by causal relations to his environment. If he neglects for too long to exercise his power of choice he ends by becoming a machine in the full sense of the word, and all possibility of free action disappears forever. He is also an animal, and like every other animal he is bound to perform during the greater part of his existence the actions needed for sustaining life.

This is one side of the picture. The other side shows man as not only a machine and' an animal but also as a being with almost unlimited possibilities of development. Among these possibilities is the acquisition of an immortal soul. Among them also is the attainment of true freedom: that is, a real and effective independence of the causal mechanism. Moreover, there is in man an innate something which tells him that these possibilities exist. Unfortunately, in the past this something has been misinterpreted as evidence that he actually has in his own right—that is, automatically and without effort on his own part—a free, independent individuality and even an immortal soul. This is not the place to trace the origin and history of the error, which is far more widely held in Western than in Eastern thought. It should be noted, however, that it is common to all prevalent views of man. The materialist who denies the existence of the soul takes for granted that if such a thing existed every man would have it automatically and as a matter of course. The spiritualist who asserts that he has a soul equally takes it for granted that he has it automatically and as a matter of course.

The consequences of this error have been disastrous for mankind, for it inevitably tends to weaken the significance of human life. He who believes that he already possesses an immortal soul can console himself with the thought that it is sufficient to avoid doing it an irreparable harm for its subsequent existence in some not undesirable state to be assured. The man who does not believe that he possesses a soul and does not even dream of the possibility of acquiring one, can live without any sense of urgency as regards the task of self-perfection, for to him it is after all only a matter of living one's life to one's satisfaction and then disappearing with all debts paid with the signing of the death certificate. For some strange reason Christian theologians, in the doctrine of vicarious atonement, have invented yet another reason for not taking life too seriously. Similarly, Buddhist theologians, in complete disregard of the teachings of their Founder, have discovered a peculiar form of solace in the doctrine of reincarnation. All such inconsequence is symptomatic of the universal human disease of "hoping for the best".

The teaching of Gurdjieff is simple and explicit. Man has the right and the obligation to earn and pay for his own being by his own conscious labour and intentional suffering. If he fails to do so he will reap the consequences and will perish either with the death of the physical body or thereafter, according to the character of his actions during life.

The conception that man is a "nothing" who can become "something" is significant not only for his ultimate destiny but also for his present life. In one sense the two are inseparable, but from a practical standpoint it would be possible to say all that it is necessary to say without referring to the soul at all. The aim of existence can be formulated in terms confined to a single lifetime. We are not free independent beings, but the slaves of our habits and the influences of our immediate environment. In our personal relations we fail very often from ignorance but still more often from complete inability to control our own behaviour. All our attempts to relieve suffering lead only to fresh suffering. All our efforts to prevent war lead only to wars more bitter and more terrible. The realization of all this should in itself be sufficient to implant in man a strong desire to change. If he sees for himself that he is not what he might be he can no longer be satisfied with himself, quite apart from any prospect of a future life. Indeed, as I have already indicated, the prospect of a future life automatically assured to him without his own efforts, will inevitably blunt the edge of his self-dissatisfaction.

We have arrived at the crucial point at which it becomes necessary—if what I am trying to express is to become clear—to leave negative criticism for a positive statement of that conception of man's nature and destiny which I hold to be true in contrast to that of either the mechanist or the spiritualist. According to Gurdjieff, man is a "nothing who can become something", a machine which can become a responsible free being. Moreover, his destiny is significant not merely for himself but for a much greater cosmic purpose which only his freedom will enable him to serve.

In order to put in its right perspective Gurdjieff's conception of man as a "nothing, who can become something," I must give some account of his teaching concerning the universal order, as follows. The universe as we know it, existing in time, has come into being by three distinct creative acts. By the first act the Creator and the Universe constitute a homogeneous system subject to the fundamental laws inherent in the very nature of time, that is, the first and second laws of thermodynamics. The Primaeval Being (named by Gurdjieff the "Sun Absolute"), existing in isolation in limitless space, radiating its own substance without any principle of regeneration, constitutes the archetype of all existence in time in its subjection to the law of inevitable degeneration and ultimate dissolution. This is the first mode of existence which always has and always will pervade the whole created universe.

The second mode of existence is that of mutually sustaining organic beings, typified in the process of eating and being eaten. Gurdjieff represents the transition as a decision of the Creator to bring about a new mode of existence which should compensate for the operation of the law of decay inherent in the very nature of time. The Sun Absolute was consequently disharmonized in such a manner as to give birth to the whole immensity of galaxies and suns. The interchange of energy between these systems and the separate modes of existence which they permit, is such as to ensure that the Sun Absolute shall not degenerate but maintain indefinitely its energy level and its being existence.

The very change in the universal order, rendered necessary if ultimate dissolution were to be averted, brought new problems due to the growing complexity of the expanding universe. The maintenance of order had been assured, but only at the expense of the need for organization. A third mode of existence thus became necessary, taking the form of individualized beings capable of bringing into the universe something which could not be placed there even by direct act of the Creator himself. This was achieved by the coming into existence of beings having the power of choice, that is, possessing to a certain degree freedom from the necessitarian laws of the Universe. Just as life depends upon a borrowing from the environment,* so does freedom itself imply a debt towards the Universe. According to Gurdjieff's conception,

* Schrödinger in *What is Life?* calls this "sucking negative entropy out of the environment."

planets throughout the universe are the place of existence of beings having the peculiar property that they are free to make or to destroy their own existence. Thus we have three modes of being, the interrelation of which constitutes the harmony of the created universe. The first is inorganic being, subject only to the laws of conservation and decay; the second is organized being with which enters the fundamental cosmic principle of eating and being eaten for the mutual sustaining of existence; the third is responsible being characterized by the power of choice.

Man, like everything else in the universe, is subject to the laws of conservation and decay. This, as I have already said, is inherent in the very nature of time. It was expressed anciently in the words of Gotama Buddha: "Impermanent are all component things. Nothing comes into existence but bears the seeds of its own dissolution." Secondly, man must eat and be eaten; like all other forms of organized life, he must serve the Great Universal Purpose for which the very sun and stars were brought into existence. Everything that eats must also be eaten. Man has no power to escape from performing his function as an apparatus for the transformation of energy however much he might wish to do so. In all this there is no question of an individual aim or purpose. Men and women, communities, the whole human race and all organic life on this and every other planet, together with the larger forms which also participate in the same process of the exchange of substance, do so without the participation of any will or purpose of their own. Nevertheless, man, while serving the great universal purpose, has the possibility at the same time of working for himself and exercising his power of choice for the sake of his own being. In the terms I have already used, this can be expressed as the creation of his own immortal soul, that is, a "something" so constituted that it is able indefinitely to withstand the law of decay and dissolution. It can also be expressed by saying that man has the possibility of becoming a free independent being, able to determine his own destiny within the limits of the general cosmic laws.

A fuller exposition of Gurdjieff's cosmological conceptions must await the publication of his own writings. Here I have tried to do no more than introduce the minimum necessary for a more exact statement of the aim and purpose of human existence.

Perhaps it will be as well to pause and make clear the distinction between power of choice and free independent being. The power of choice is exercised only "here and now." It is the ability, to give an instance, to choose between saying yes or no to a specific stimulus to action. It does not extend to processes operating over a period of time. The reason for this is that man himself has no permanent existence: he is a mere succession of momentary selves. Each one of these selves can, but very seldom does, exercise the power of saying yes or no to the possibility of an action arising either from the man's own automatism or from a stimulus exerted from without. Free independent being implies vastly more than this. It implies, first, the possession of a permanent conscious individuality without which there can be no freedom. It implies, secondly, the power to stand outside or above the automatism of our bodily existence as a mechanic stands outside or above a machine. Moreover, this "standing outside" must not be that of a passive spectator who is able to watch but not control the working of the machine. Much confusion on this point has entered the thought of those who have dabbled in Eastern notions and have been impressed by the doctrine of non-attachment. It has been interpreted to mean that a merely passive contemplation of external activity is an end in itself. Non-attachment of this kind has certain uses, but only as one element out of many which are involved in the attainment of free individuality.

One example may serve to make the distinction clear. The ordinary average man has no power of conscious control over his own emotional state. He is sad, cheerful, bored, excited, interested, astonished, irritated, worried, angry, jealous, grieved and joyful by turns under the influence of automatic associations and formed habits combined with the passing stimulus of the external situation. He is moved by desire or aversion and regards these states as the natural expression of his own being. But, should they happen to come in conflict with some equally definite mental attitude a struggle ensues the outcome of which depends in its turn upon quite accidental factors, such as fear of the consequences of the desired action or slavery to the opinions of others. It is the same whether his emotions are violent and tempestuous, or feeble and ineffectual. In all cases they arise, manifest and disappear according to a process which he does not understand and certainly cannot control. Naturally, he does not realize this because his early training has developed in him habits of repressing certain outward manifestations not considered to be "good form" in the particular environment in which he belongs. He has been taught to call this repression "self-control." He is not aware that these feelings which he hides nevertheless determine his state and colour his actions in another and, for his own being often hot less harmful, form.

The pernicious habit of attaching importance only to that which is evident to the eyes of others and not to one's own inner state, develops in people an impulse of self-justification which operates so automatically that they can nearly always feel themselves to be in the right. By this process many undesirable emotional reactions can pass quite unnoticed by the person concerned, with the result that he fails also to see his inability to control them.

Now control itself may mean several things. I have already referred to the automatic "control" due simply to habit or the operation of some kind of fear. It is virtually the only kind of control which can exist in the ordinary average man or woman. There is a different kind of control which comes from the practice of non-attachment. It must be understood at once that this is exceedingly difficult to acquire. It is by no means simply a matter of change of mental altitude. By long and persistent efforts, mainly concerned with acquiring the ability to direct attention, it is possible to gain the power to withdraw attention from a given stimulus and so avoid responding to it. This may be done, for example, by focusing attention sufficiently on some selected point and thereby detaching it from the emotional stimulus. By such means a man may acquire the ability to weaken or extinguish any undesired emotional state. He may do this deliberately for the specific purpose of liberating himself from slavery to his emotions, or he may do it without set purpose as part of some religious exercise of act of devotion. In the latter case the effort to focus attention is directed towards God or some saint conceived as an object of worship. Various degrees and various kinds of non-attachment can be achieved from this kind of practice. They confer a certain degree of inner strength, but not true inner freedom.

The reason for this is that they do not bring with them the power intentionally to determine what emotional state shall be present. For example, a man may attain a considerable degree of non-attachment and yet be unable to be astonished simply by deciding to be so. To have control over one's emotions implies not only the power to feel what one wants to feel, but also and even more, the power to feel what one does not want to feel. Since the emotional state is one of the decisive factors in determining the behaviour of the physical organism, no man can be entirely free until he is able to have, at any given moment and to the degree of intensity which he judges to be necessary, the emotion appropriate to the behaviour that he decides to manifest. In writing these words, I am not unaware of the misunderstanding to which they may give rise, for many people who are in reality complete slaves to their own automatism claim with every appearance of sincerity that they can feel what they choose to feel. For example, they believe that they can be angry because they deem anger appropriate to a given situation and can be this without (as they call it) "giving way" to the anger. All this is illusory, and the very fact that such self-deception is possible, is one of the main obstacles which prevent people understanding their true situation.

For anyone who is capable of even a small degree of impartial self-observation the situation is fully expressed in the words of St. Paul which I have already quoted: "For that which I do I allow not: for what I would, that do I not; but what I hate, that do I." The fundamental postulate which I have been trying to set out plainly is: this situation can be changed and a man can become a free independent being with full power over himself and all his reactions, mental, emotional and physical. The achievement of freedom is only one aspect, for the real significance of freedom lies in the use that is made of it. I have already made it clear that, according to Gurdjieff's conception of

human destiny, the man who has become free has an
unlimited responsibility towards his fellow-men in
their own struggle for freedom and towards his Creator
in the accomplishment of the Divine purpose.

How far is the ordinary average man on the way to
the fulfilment of this great destiny? With what does he
occupy his life?

What are the motives which in fact determine his
actions? In order to answer this, we must bear in mind
the three modes of being possible in the Universe. Man
is first of all a material object and like all material
objects his existence is subject to the laws of thermodynamics. He cannot "by taking thought add one
cubit to his stature." Also, he must grow old and his
body must die and return to the dust. This is the first
aspect of all being. Secondly, he must also fulfil the
functions of animal existence. He cannot escape from
the obligation to provide for the needs of his animal
body. These, whether he likes it or not, must take a
considerable proportion of his time and strength. In
all these ways he is in no wise different from other
animals. The real significance of his life turns upon
whether or not he devotes his surplus time and surplus
energy to a purpose higher than his animal existence.
If he does not do so, he is no more than a thinking
animal.

To make a right assessment we must enumerate
the types of purpose which cannot be called
"higher than" those of animal life. Such are all

purposes directed to the satisfaction of egoistical desires. Such also are all actions with no aim at all, all actions which can be comprised under the general description of "killing time"—such as the occupation of leisure in an entirely passive state with what are rightly called "distractions." Recreation is necessary for the man who is engaged upon intensive work, including the intensive work required for the creation of his own being. It is not, however, in itself a purpose higher than his animal existence, but rather an inevitable consequence of the limitations of his own strength. It provides a man with a certain amount of food necessary for his inner growth but it is not, and in itself cannot be, described as a "higher purpose."

Apart from egoistic and unworthy activities and apart also from habitual and mechanical activities not directly connected with the animal life, it is obvious that the ordinary average man does very often do things to attain an aim beyond his animal nature. For example, he is not satisfied with bringing his children into the world and allowing them to reach manhood or womanhood as mere animals, but wishes to see them "well educated"—which should mean, free responsible individuals. He may make considerable sacrifices for the attainment of this aim, but if he does not understand what is involved and what is required, if in fact he allows his children to grow up unconscious slaves without the possibility of further development, he has done no better for them than an animal does for its young. The right understanding of this is so important that I devote the next chapter to it.

Another type of non-animal activity is the acquisition of knowledge for purposes other than the satisfaction of animal needs. The desire to know oneself, to know the universe and to know one's destiny in the universe is certainly a noble desire. Labours directed towards these attainments are very far removed from those of mere animal life. I need hardly ask how much they occupy of the time and forces of the ordinary average man. The really serious question is, whether those who imagine that they occupy themselves with Objective Science are genuinely devoted to this aim or whether they are moved for the most part by the same passions— ambition, emulation and the desire for external reward— that enter as a taint into all human activity. Philosophers themselves do not fail to emphasize the spirit of disinterested inquiry and the detachment from personal considerations which are indispensable in the pursuit of truth. The history of philosophy does not, on the whole, show that philosophers have been exempt from the ordinary human passions. I have used the words "on the whole" because there have been noteworthy exceptions in men like Socrates and Spinoza whose lives demonstrate something of what can be achieved by the disinterested pursuit of truth combined with a resolute struggle with oneself. But the question of philosophers' motives is less important than that of the results of their labours. Our Western thought runs in channels dug for us chiefly by philosophers in the line of succession of the ancient Greeks. About this and about the claims made on behalf of natural science to furnish objective truths, I write in the third chapter.

There is finally the aim of religion. As has often been said, this aim, above all others, is one by which a man is differentiated from an animal. But it is true only when the aim is a live one, and when religion is something more than a refuge from suffering or a half-hearted insurance against the possibility of a day of reckoning. It is possible to engage in practices ostensibly religious from motives which to all intents and purposes are animal motives, such as the enjoyment of ritual or the desire for a particular kind of emotional stimulus. The small part played by any genuine religious beliefs and aspirations in determining human action throughout the world at the present time is one of the principal reasons why it is difficult to regard modern man as very much more than a thinking animal. Religion is the subject matter of the fourth chapter.

In the title of this chapter I have placed in antithesis the terms, Thinking Animal and Reasonable Being. A reasonable being is one who can be relied upon to act in every given situation according to the dictates of objective reason. Were mankind composed even in a small proportion of such beings the situation of the world would not be that which our eyes behold today.

CHAPTER II

EDUCATION—HOW PEOPLE ARE DEPRIVED
OF THEIR SOULS

WHEN a man really understands that he is not what he might be, a corresponding desire for "being" will begin to appear. The feeling of the need for being—or hunger for being—is not easy to describe to anyone who has never felt his own emptiness, who is confident that he is his own master, who believes that he can control his own behaviour by his own "will." So strong are the influences which lead us to believe that we are free individuals that we can only with great difficulty come to recognise the extent of our mechanicalness. For this it is necessary to acquire a certain capacity for objective self-observation and for sincerity with oneself. With this capacity comes a power of discriminating between real and illusory aims. The primary real aim of a man who begins to sense his own helplessness and slavery must be to create in himself something reliable, free and able to take and carry out independent decisions. But so long as a man remains under the illusion that he already possesses these things without having, worked for them, the distinction between real and illusory aims does not arise. Not feeling himself in want of being his desires are directed outwards towards the attainment of purposes which "appeal to him" for a variety of reasons. Through the resulting external activity his attention is diverted from his own inward emptiness and he is able to live without suspecting that he is missing everything that is of ultimate value in human existence. What he calls the success or the failure of his enterprises serve equally to hypnotize him. He attributes one or the other to his own cleverness or stupidity, energy or laziness, strength or weakness of purpose and to the well-intentioned and ill-intentioned actions of other people. In other words, he interprets his experience in terms of intentions and their fulfilment. It is true that he sees the action of various external and incalculable factors and he may even believe in such things as good and bad luck. What he does not see is that the whole process of human intercourse is a great puppet-show, in which none of the actors is- free from the strings which produce his every movement; a puppet-show, moreover, in which there is no showman but only the accidental combinations of uncoordinated lines of cause and effect.

In the last chapter of this book I give a brief outline of Gurdjieff's answer to the obvious question which arises: "Why, if we are puppets, do we not feel the strings?" Here I must start with the situation of the man who realizes that he is not what he might be and experiences, in consequence, the beginning of the desire *to be*. If he then asks himself: "How can I *be*? What are the conditions which make it possible *to be*?" he will realize that, at least, it implies the power to take and act upon a decision which is not imposed upon him by external forces. He must be capable of maintaining an objective attitude towards himself. He must have, the strength to make efforts by his own free decision and not imposed by external forces or the promptings of his own vanity and self-importance. He must not be afraid of the unknown; for his journey towards *being* will inevitably lead him into unfamiliar situations which may completely upset all that he thinks he understands about himself and the world in which he lives. Finally, he must not shrink from suffering, but look upon it as the very coinage in which he will pay for his own becoming.

If all these things are a condition for making a start upon the way of being, one may well despair and echo the words: "Who then shall be saved?"

Thinking impartially about this situation, we cannot fail to see that the possibility of being depends upon preparation—which no man can effect by himself any more than anyone, with the doubtful exception of Baron Munchausen, could pull himself out of the mud by his own hair. Moreover, it should be obvious that this preparation can be made only during the formative years when the whole stock of associations which determine the possible experiences of after-life are implanted in the fresh, receptive brain system of the growing child. There is, therefore, an obligation which each generation owes to the next, of preparing children to become responsible beings, capable of objective judgment, and understanding that everything that is real must be paid for and that conscious labour and intentional suffering are the sole means whereby payment can be made. Such understanding does not arise spontaneously. It requires teaching reinforced by example. The child is helpless and dependent, and unless this work is honestly done for him by his parents and teachers he will reach adult age defective in that one thing which is needed if he is to fulfil his destiny in a becoming manner.

It must be admitted that if the upbringing of a child is seriously defective in respect of these essential requirements, that child will, through no fault of his own, be deprived of the possibility of becoming what he should be. It is difficult to describe the tragic situation of a being who, as regards natural disposition and other hereditary factors, is perfectly capable of attaining real being and yet, as a result of a defective upbringing and bad example, is unable either to understand what is necessary for him, or to make and carry out the decision to work on himself. No one who begins to understand this even in a small degree can fail to realize that the preparation of the next generation for responsible age is a sacred obligation and must form one of the aims of every normal person.

The aim of education can be formulated in terms which I believe would receive fairly general assent, even from those who have not yet begun to think of human destiny as involving the change of being. We might, for example, write: "The aim of education is to produce an independent human being, understanding his obligation towards himself and towards the world in which he lives, feeling the necessity to fulfil that obligation and capable of making the efforts and sacrifices necessary to fulfil it.' Now what in fact does contemporary humanity do in order to bring into existence a new generation able to understand and fulfil its obligations? Children are conceived, very often unwillingly, still more often unintentionally, by people who do not even try to understand the extraordinary event they are bringing about. When children are born they are subjected almost from birth to influences which will inevitably produce in them such characteristics as vanity, self-will, self-importance, distrust, deceitfulness, suggestibility, dependence upon other people and, at the very root and centre of their being, egoism. When one watches parents with their own children one is almost tempted to believe that it is their calculated intention to bring about these results. They proceed by a mixture of flattery and cajolery, repression and scolding. By their own inconstant behaviour they form in the child corresponding habitual responses of inconstancy. By praising and blaming always in relation to external actions and visible manifestations, they extinguish in the child the natural feeling of the importance of that which goes on in his inward experience. Neglecting the inward life—except by stuffing the child with every kind of absurdity—they do everything possible to establish the conviction that it is what we appear to be, and not what we are, that is important. Children are made to think and to feel, by influences which are brought to bear on them almost from birth, that it is only their external manifestations seen by other people, which determine their value. Activity not seen by other people, either because it goes on in their inner experience or because it proceeds out of sight of others, ceases to be matter for self-satisfaction or shame. This process is intensively continued so long as children remain in contact with their parents and their nurses. In some cases, the emphasis is upon flattery and undeserved praise directed to even the most trivial gestures. In others it is upon a harsh repression of outward manifestations not conforming to some artificial code of behaviour. Sometimes, even, the first kind of influence is brought to bear by one parent and the second by the other. There is no essential difference in the consequences except to alter the balance between vanity and deceitfulness, self-will and distrust, and all the other characteristic elements in the psyche of the average man and woman. For it must be clearly understood that what is done in childhood produces its effects throughout life. The seeds of vanity sown even before a child begins to speak can produce a harvest which will disfigure his life and ruin his chances of self-creation.

The child next enters into some kind of community—a school or the society of other children— and new factors come into play. The strongest influence which is now brought to bear is subservience to and dread of the opinion of others. As soon as he enters into a life in which there is a community of other children the child begins to be the slave of what is called "public opinion." This slavery takes hold of him more and more and becomes one of the dominating factors which control his actions throughout the rest of his life. He is unable to do anything without being influenced in one way or another by the thought of the effect of his actions on the opinion of other people who will be aware of them. His whole life begins to be divided into two parts. One consists of his external manifestations seen by other people. It is all the same whether this dependence upon other people takes the form of subservience or revolt, whether he is concerned to please or to shock. It is the same because in either case the possibility of inward independence and an inward free judgment is stifled. The other part is that of his unseen life, in which he allows every kind of pernicious habit—mental, emotional and physical—to develop in him and crystallize, with little or no sense of shame or realization of the harmful consequences for himself.

A second kind of influence present in almost every educational system is the stimulus to effort not through inner decision but through competition and reward. To be better, not only in the necessary things—which have to be learned and where there might be some excuse for making use of this stimulus to effort— but also in even entirely artificial activities (such as sports and games and various other social ornaments by which no useful purpose is served) becomes for the child something important in itself and is associated in his mind with the very aim of existence. The child is taught that it matters that he should have pre-eminence over others, and particularly that kind of pre-eminence which is visible and assessed in terms of some external, stereotyped criterion. The results persist throughout life and give rise to strange and abnormal conditions in people, such as ambition, the desire for praise, the urge to dominate and be important, all of which exercise a most baleful influence on the possibility of normal human relationships.

Thus everything is done to enhance the importance of appearance and diminish the importance of reality. Therefore, what need to have an objectively satisfied attitude towards oneself inwardly? Of genuinely unbiased self-approval there is only talk. No effective steps are taken to develop in children the realization that one's own impartial judgment of oneself, made inwardly, without reference to the good or bad opinions of other people, should be the basis of one's own actions. This, though sometimes theoretically discussed, does not enter effectively into any form of education.

These are not the only artificial and pernicious influences which are brought to bear from early childhood and continue all through the critical period in which a child is being prepared for his adult life. Another such influence—and this applies to the majority of countries of this (so-called) modern civilization of ours, and particularly to the English-speaking countries—is a very strange attitude towards sex. Adults find it in some way undesirable or embarrassing to explain to children quite necessary things, not only about the physiology of the human sex functions but also about the part that sex plays or should play in the life of man. Owing to this peculiar embarrassment over one of the things that it is most essential children should not approach with embarrassment but understanding, there arises a whole series of very undesirable consequences. One of these is concealment of every kind in connection with sexual activities and, associated with it, the development of pernicious habits such as masturbation and juvenile sexual intercourse which have decisive evil consequences for the whole of adult life. A second is the combined result of concealment as regards sex and the dread of the attitude of other people. This very often prevents young men and women from entering into normal sexual relationships at marriage, with the result that they are deprived of the benefits of that process of mutual completion which is necessary for the normal existence of bisexual beings. And finally, there arises a mental and emotional obsession with the sexual act itself that is peculiarly harmful for the formation of a free independent individuality.

As regards the actual, teaching which forms the ostensible purpose of education, the subjects taught and the methods employed are taken without any real understanding of the needs of adult life. Nothing is taught about the nature of man, about what he is and what he might become. Nothing of real significance is conveyed concerning the obligations which a man has towards himself and towards his fellow-men.

Only accidentally, and then on the basis of egoistic emulation, is anything done to develop strength of purpose in relation to one's own body, the power to withstand fatigue and pain and to make even a simple and natural use of one's bodily functions. As regards the needs of the emotional life, something worse than ignorance prevails. The very idea that unbiased emotional judgment can be made only if something is formed by a correct development of the emotional functions, is not understood at all. This is particularly serious, since the ability to acquire mind-knowledge through writing and other methods of transmission which are now very generally available is a positive danger unless it is balanced with an equal degree of development of a power of critical judgment.

The things that are taught are often strange and even ludicrous; they have no bearing at all upon the way in which the subsequent life of the boy or girl will be spent. When I asked recently about a boy's homework I was told that he was learning as his history lesson the dates of all the battles in the English Civil War. Is it possible to conceive a more useless activity during that period in the life of a young man when there is so much that it is essential for him to learn? Apart from the absurdity of learning by heart "facts," with no reference to their significance or interpretation, there are many kinds of intellectual disciplines (so-called) which are taught in a way that has very serious after-consequences—that is, they are taught without reference to any concrete reality. The result is that into the very mechanism of thought there enters an inability to distinguish between words and the meaning for which they stand. Children taught in this way are deprived in after-life of the possibility of normal concrete thinking and, being able only to juggle with words, they fall defenceless victims of catch phrases which they accept without even delaying to ask whether they correspond to anything real.

Even at the best, only perfunctory attempts are made to arouse in children the desire to understand meanings and not be satisfied just with the sound of words. Since, however, some kind of meaning has to exist for the child's own subjective processes, everyone attributes to the words he hears the particular subjective meaning which happens to arise in him at the moment or a meaning which is suggested to him by some kind of propaganda.

Let us take one discipline, mathematics, which contributes to the growth of this unreality in thought. For a special historical reason mathematics has enjoyed great prestige since Grecian times. This subject is taught without any reference to the ability, which is comparatively rare, to understand and make effective use of the abstract operations involved. But since the capacity for imitation is very strong in children, and they are able to learn by rote quite complicated things without understanding their meaning, a deceptive appearance of intellectual apprehension can result. Moreover, it is usually not observed that many of the operations of mathematics require only motor reflexes and can be performed without any real understanding of their meaning. Thus boys and girls apparently can become proficient in mathematics without understanding anything whatever of the logical processes involved or the nature of abstract thinking. Those who do rebel against this meaningless activity are simply described as "bad at mathematics."

To witness the teaching of languages in almost any school in almost any country is a painful experience for one who realizes the liberating effect of grasping the thought processes of an alien race. Among nearly all European peoples, the teaching of foreign languages is confined to closely similar languages of the same European group. So children grow up quite unaware of the special limitations imposed by the linguistic form to which they are accustomed upon the possibility of giving expression to certain important kinds of experience. The Semitic languages, for example, have a far greater power than the European of fixing attention upon the meaning of words, owing to the constancy of the basic significance of each triliteral root. To take part with Arabs in their seemingly interminable discussions about meanings is to understand by comparison how little Europeans are concerned with the import of what they say. The agglutinative languages of Central Asia (and I believe also Chinese: though I do not know Chinese) have a singular power of expressing fine shades of difference regarding the degree of conscious intention involved in an action. Now it is a fundamental principle that the value of every action is in direct proportion to the degree of conscious intention with which it is performed, and it is therefore probably no accident that for thousands of years Central Asia has been that part of the world where the real nature of man is best understood. The European approach to the Semitic and Turanian languages is characteristically absurd. When for some reason these languages are taught to Europeans who have to work in Eastern countries, a fictitious Indo-European grammatical form is imposed which disguises their true structure, and they are learned quite superficially without any conception of their real power. Only in very rare instances do Europeans through intimate contact with these races come into possession of the unsuspected treasury of practical wisdom enshrined in their languages.

The ordinary teaching of languages is as far removed from these things as is a Lyons Corner House from the Taj Mahal. Not only do the great majority of children grow up without the ability to think in even one foreign language, but they also waste years without so much as acquiring the ability to make themselves understood in the simplest everyday concern. Their acquaintance with foreign literature never extends to those works in which the characteristic thought of another race is expressed, and even when it is carried, far enough to enable them to pass what are called higher examinations they do so almost exclusively through learning by heart passages which they do not attempt to understand and a mass of useless data about the dates and lives and presumed interrelations of the various authors and their schools.

Throughout all the different disciplines of school education runs one common thread: neglect of concrete meanings and reliance solely upon the ability to juggle with words. This is encouraged very strongly by the evaluation of results of effort through oral and written examinations which no-one attempts to relate to any inner understanding. One tragic effect of the whole process is the appearance throughout the world of millions of people completely defenceless against verbal suggestion. By the whole process of what is called education we form men and women incapable of free independent existence and more and more dependent upon external support in almost the whole activity of their lives. This applies equally to the work they are obliged to undertake in order to earn their living and to the use of the leisure forced upon them by their inability to employ themselves. Whether they are clerks in banks or workers in factories they rely on an entirely mechanized life in order to be as free as may be from the necessity for any independent decision. When their work stops they simply pass to another condition of dependence for the whole of their recreation. They remain passive in relation to stereotyped external stimuli—cinematograph shows or football games or whatever it may be—or else they indulge in the most remarkable forms of mechanized activity such as the spending of hours in filling up forms for football pools and the like, and this at a period when it might well be supposed that the filling in of forms would have become a most distasteful activity. More and more people are becoming dependent upon government and upon being governed, increasingly requiring that their lives be regulated for them. Another curious phenomenon of today is that where this regulation is not performed for them by governments it is undertaken by advertising agents. In the United States almost the entire life of man is regulated and controlled by advertisements. From the moment when men and women wake up in the morning until they go to bed at night almost everything that they will do or refrain from doing is virtually determined for them. It is determined by the simple process of suggesting, by reiterated statements in very simple language, that such and such a thing will make them well or happy or even, nowadays, that it is conducive to the American way of life. In all this the advertisers, with a faith always justified by the result, rely upon the absence of any personal initiative or power to resist reiterated suggestion.

Universal suggestibility has also made the peoples of the world defenceless against political propaganda. It is particularly distressing to see how this operates as a result of even a small dose of "education" among the masses of such countries as India and Russia, where through the weapon of mass suggestion small groups can wield almost unlimited power. In our modern civilization, (as it is called) people are subject to political propaganda or the suggestions of advertising agents: whether they live in so-called free countries or under what are named dictatorships, the situation is entirely the same. No free individuals exist; everywhere people's lives are determined and governed by a series of stereotyped external stimuli against which they have no resistance at all. And the direct cause of all this is our so-called education. By the process of this education men and women are produced who are perfectly adapted to a mechanized existence. Almost the only effective attainment which the great majority of people acquire in the process of education is the ability to read—an ability which is the greatest possible misfortune for any person who is highly suggestible and who has not had developed in him the power of independent critical judgment. Further, education has made possible a special process which serves more than any other to divorce people from any contact with reality. This process is modern journalism.

Modern newspapers are divided mainly into three parts—advertisement, sport and news. I have already referred to the slavery induced in everyday life through exposure to advertisement suggestion. The ability to read about sport induces another peculiar and dangerous passivity in the use of leisure. It leads also to a quite artificial system of values whereby men who have acquired some special physical skill are accorded the status of national heroes. I should not, of course, omit from this reference to artificial hero-worship the "build-up" of cinema stars and other particularly

automatized, helpless individuals, whose owners
use them for expressing entirely unreal situations
and emotions and for stimulating an artificial sexual
response in very large numbers of people at a small
cost. The third item called "news" exercises a most
peculiar influence on human life. Almost invariably
the news items in newspapers are inaccurate, and
especially^ so when important events are concerned.
The information they contain is never that which is
most relevant, but that which is either sensational or
calculated to induce in the reader the particular attitude
towards events that the owners and editors (usually
quite unconscious of any intentional bias) believe to
be desirable. Thus when war was imminent in 1939,
hardly any newspaper in the world gave its. readers a
true picture of the situation. The fact that at the present
time a completely false picture of the world economic
situation is current derives largely from the desire of
almost every newspaper, to avoid giving "news" which
will depress trade or destroy confidence in currencies.

I have endeavoured to give an impartial description
of what is called "education" and the consequences
of the behaviour which we manifest towards children
from birth right up to the time when it becomes
necessary that they should be free independent beings.
Not only is the totality of these influences disastrous
for ordinary everyday life, but it is also still more
dreadful in its effect upon the possibility of acquiring
a soul. By soul, I mean that something in a man which

should be himself, that something which should be free, independent, able to resist suggestion, able to take decisions and persevere in them. It is to ensure the possession of this something that above all else the efforts of those responsible for the upbringing of children should be directed, and it is precisely that which the process of education does not supply.

Perhaps I should refer at this stage to what are called "progressive schools," the ostensible aim of which is precisely to encourage the child to "be himself." This is almost invariably done by depriving the child of guidance and restraint just when guidance and restraint are necessary, while exposing him to the influences which I have called "public opinion," namely, the accidental prejudices and conventions of the community of children of Which the institution is composed. Moreover, a child, having left his parents with the seeds already sown in him of egoism, vanity, self-importance, distrust, deceitfulness and the rest, finds in the so-called "free" conditions of a progressive school fertile ground for a vicious harvest which differs from that of other educational establishments only in showing a somewhat less attractive balance between concealment and ostentation.

Now in order to envisage perhaps a little of what there should be, and might be, in the process of his formation as a responsible man or woman, let us turn our attention to the real situation of the human being. By formation I mean the transition from the moment of conception to the moment of what should be free independent existence. In order to make the process clear I must refer again to Gurdjieff's teaching with regard to the nature of man. According to this teaching man has what he terms three, independent "spiritualised parts" or, more simply, three brains. With one man thinks, with one he feels and with one he senses. They. are called independent spiritualised parts to indicate that each one can become a centre of experience. Each has its own way of perceiving the world and reacting to it. In a properly balanced human being each of the three parts contributes one indispensable element to the totality of his understanding and the effectiveness of his action. The human being in whom one or more of these parts is abnormally developed—or, as is more frequently the case, neglected and left undeveloped—can have only lop-sided, incomplete reactions to the World. Since for its normal development each part requires a special kind of training, any rightly conceived system of education must, as one of its primary objectives, attempt to ensure that this balance is achieved and maintained.

To grasp what is involved it must be understood that each of the three brains corresponds to a certain nervous mechanism. The thinking brain has its seat almost entirely in the cerebral hemispheres. It makes use of the familiar processes of association and disjunction which lead to the experience of affirmation and negation applied to presentations in the form of words and other symbols. It operates at any given moment with an infinitesimal fraction of the totality of pre-formed associative material stored in the memory from early childhood. In one sense it is a very complicated mechanism, but in another it is a very simple one for in the end the whole of its activity is reduced to the words "yes" and "no". The feeling brain operates quite differently, without words, in terms of the total affective experience of the given moment. The entire condition of the organism reflects itself in the activity of the sympathetic nervous system, which is the mechanism of the feeling brain. Pleasure and suffering, desire and aversion, approval and disapproval all arise in us more or less independently of our thinking—except insofar as mental associations sometimes automatically arouse emotional associations. We are seldom directly aware of the activity proceeding in our feeling brain, which belongs to what is called the unconscious or subconscious regions of the human psyche. The sensing brain is situated in that part which determines all our reflexes and many of our motor activities: the spinal cord and certain of the ganglia at the base of the skull and in the frontal lobes.

In a normal human individual each of these three parts is capable of conscious experience but, largely owing to the harmful conditions of early childhood and subsequent abnormal education, children grow up so that their feeling and sensing brains disappear from their ordinary consciousness and fall into their subconscious. They are thus led to relate their own Existence to one part only, the thinking brain, to the experience of which they attach the word "self" or "I". Nevertheless, the other two parts continue to act in them and have a decisive influence upon their behaviour. They are the source of many of our motives and because we do not understand their action a great deal of our behaviour is incomprehensible to ourselves and to other people. If we observe ourselves even a little objectively, we constantly find ourselves performing actions the source of which cannot be derived from what we may be thinking about at the moment and even may go entirely against the views and attitudes which have been formed in our thinking part. I do not propose to discuss further the three brains and the means which should be used to ensure their full harmonious development. These things will be fully dealt with when Gurdjieff's writings become accessible to those who seriously wish to study his ideas.

The psychic constitution of man is not fully described in terms of the three brains alone. In addition, a man should have a fourth part independent of the three brains: his own "I". This should be formed in him by the time he reaches what Gurdjieff terms responsible age. Only the man who possesses an "I" can make independent judgments and be able to stand up against external influences, resist external suggestions and above all make impartial self-judgments. It is only through such impartial—or, as Gurdjieff says, conscious—self-judgments that a man can undertake the work to which I referred in the previous chapter: the acquiring of his own being.

It is not at all easy to convey what is meant by having an "I" or being oneself. I have tried to show elsewhere* that the arguments by which people try to convince themselves that they have such an "I" are fallacious, that all that can be observed is a succession of partial selves, often trivial and always impermanent. A man who "does not know his own mind," who cannot make decisions, valid for all his moods and all external circumstances, cannot be said to possess an "I". All that can be said of him is that outwardly he is one: he has one body, one name and a general behaviour pattern which other people recognize. But there is no inward unity corresponding to this external self. It is true that a man speaks of himself as "I". He is interested in and cares about himself and expects attention and consideration for this self of his; he is offended when it is slighted and flattered when it is praised. The non-existent "something" which is the Object of all this solicitude can be called his Imaginary I, or more simply, his egoism. Egoism is the imaginary substitute for a man's real self. To have a real "I" is incompatible with egoism and egoism is incompatible with a real "I". Unfortunately, it is egoism and not a real "I" that is formed in children by parental attention and the kind of education which I have described. From earliest childhood a future responsible being is encouraged to think in terms of "mine," "I" want, "I" will, "I" won't. Impulses

* See *The Crisis in Human Affairs*, by J.G. Bennett. 1948. Hoddder & Stoughton Chapter III [Now available in both print and digital form. Ed.]

of this kind are not natural, nor are they inherent in children, but they arise and rapidly gain force because devoted parents and loving nurses find some kind of attraction in these egoistic manifestations. They do not see in them the precursors of very disagreeable qualities which will persist throughout life unless later eradicated by conscious labour and intentional suffering.

To have an aim in life chosen by oneself on the basis of one's own self-judgment and not as the result of accidental influences or deliberate suggestion from without, is one mark of a real "I". To be able to make self-imposed efforts for the attainment of such an aim without the stimulus of anything either feared or hoped for from other people, is another mark. It follows that a real "I" cannot develop in a child who becomes subservient to public opinion whether by way of submission or revolt. Vanity is a special form of subservience to the opinion of others which prevents the growth of any true individuality, and yet vanity is fostered in children by every word of unmerited praise or flattery which they hear from, the day they begin to become aware of the attitude of other people towards them.

A real "I" comes from struggle: but the struggle must proceed from within. It must be based upon an inner standard of conduct combined with a capacity for impartial self-judgment. It cannot come from struggle induced by any external stimulus from either hope or fear of anything which the outside world can give or do.

The development of such a power in a child can come only from the growth of his own understanding reinforced by the example of those older people with whom he is in contact. What hope can there be for a child when those responsible for his upbringing do not know how to develop his understanding and show by their own example that they act from every possible motive except impartial self-judgment? And so it comes about that extremely few children reach manhood or womanhood with anything corresponding to a real "I" or with any realization of the obligation which is inherent in the possession of freedom to say "yes" or "no" to one's own destiny.

This brings me to the last general negative feature of virtually all educational systems of the present time, namely, the inculcation of the doctrine that to exist is to have rights. To anyone who has an objective understanding of the real situation this is a pernicious doctrine fraught with terrible consequences for the individual and for the race. The exact contrary is true: to exist is to be under obligation. In so far as I exist as a being with any degree of freedom I have borrowed something from the universe, since my freedom is necessarily at the expense of the universe itself. The something I have borrowed, namely, my own freedom, I am under obligation to repay. I can evade the obligation by abandoning my freedom, by merging and disappearing into the undifferentiated totality of things. That course is quite open to me; and it is the one followed by the great majority of people. But if I desire to be I must recognise that existence is something which has to be paid for. Those doctrines which teach anything contrary to this and thus encourage people to believe that they have rights which they are entitled to secure at the expense of others, are more responsible than is anything else for the generally disastrous condition of human life at the present time.

In defining the aim of education at the beginning of this chapter I used the expression, "understanding his obligation towards himself and towards the world in which he lives." The obligation can be accepted and fulfilled only by the man or woman who has a real "I". In so far as education fails in this aim, it betrays its duty. There can be no general improvement in the condition of the world until this is understood and made the basis of every educational system.

CHAPTER III

SCIENCE AND PHILOSOPHY—THE

FOUNT OF UNWISDOM

IN the two foregoing chapters I have tried to show that it is unnecessary to invoke any theological or cosmological theories in order to convince oneself that there is something profoundly unsatisfactory about the present-day life of man, and that the only hope of an improvement lies in redressing the balance between man's power over himself and his power over nature. I have not disguised my own conviction that to understand the human situation it is necessary to see it in the wider perspective of a universal purpose; and I have also tried to show how this purpose is conceived according to Gurdjieff's ideas upon which the present book is explicitly based. Many people consider it quite legitimate, whenever any views about God and the Universe are expressed, to ask the question: "How do you know about this? Can it be scientifically proved?" —implying that scientific proof is a well-established and infallible procedure. The notion that science is competent to pronounce judgment upon ultimate questions seems to be so widely held that before going further, it is advisable to devote one chapter to an examination of the claims of science to provide us with reliable knowledge about ourselves and the world in which we live.

I shall use the term, Science, to denote the whole group of processes directed to the acquisition of knowledge by the exclusive use of sense perceptions, with intellectual analyses of the data given in sense perception and inference (inductive and deductive) from the results of these analyses. I shall regard as excluded from the domain of science the data of purely subjective experience, including any kind of inspired cognition or revelation. In drawing this distinction, I should make it clear that I have taken it from what appear to be the currently held views concerning what is scientific and what unscientific. It fails to allow for one indispensable element in scientific activity, and that is the "leap in the dark" by which a new hypothesis is formulated. This reservation is not important for our present purpose since most people will recognise the general distinction I have made. It may help to avoid misunderstanding, however, if I say at this point that in criticizing science as we know it I do not wish to suggest that valid knowledge cannot be attained through observation and inference, but rather that as far as the really important subjects of man and his place in the universe are concerned we have been making the wrong observations and drawing the wrong conclusions.

Science today enjoys a high degree of prestige. Although it occupies less of the average person's time than sport, the cinema, political discussion or reading the newspaper, it nevertheless remains in the background as the main pillar which supports our faith in progress and the superiority of our Western civilization over both past and contemporary civilizations. In so far as the average person believes in anything, he believes in science. Moreover, in so far as he refuses to believe in something or other it is because he assumes that that something or other is unscientific or cannot be scientifically proved. This is not really a new situation for it has existed since the rise of Greek philosophy. For more than a thousand years even devout people have considered it unreasonable to believe in God unless one could produce "proof" of His existence. In discussing the claims of science to possess the sole means of acquiring valid knowledge we must include with science all those schools of philosophical thought which claim to derive their authority from the same source.

One more distinction must be made before we can embark upon our enquiry. I have defined science as a group of processes for the acquisition of knowledge. This divides it from technology defined as a group of processes for acting upon the external world. When this distinction is drawn we can see at once that the prestige of science is derived largely not from science itself but from technology. We are impressed above all by the achievements of the technologist. Most people assume that technology is based on science: we first know and then do. They point to many modern industries which have their origin in scientific research. The success of these industries in placing new and undreamed of powers at the disposal of man is regarded in some way as validating science itself.

We say: "Look at the steam engine; look at the motor car; look at the wireless; look at all the achievements of chemical industry: how can you deny that science is more entitled to our respect than all these ancient traditions which have done nothing comparable to raise the standards of human life?" The accusation is levelled against science that it has been even more successful in developing weapons of destruction than arts of peace, that the progress of technology has raised new grim economic problems that did not exist in a simpler society. I am not concerned with this kind of criticism of science; for it is a perfectly valid reply to claim neutrality in these matters on behalf of the scientific activity and to say that it is the people who misuse the results of science that are to blame for the resultant troubles. This is simply one aspect of the situation, to which I have several times referred, wherein we find ourselves with no moral progress corresponding to our increased technical powers.

My purpose in making the distinction between science and technology is to draw attention to one point often overlooked: the assumption, to which I have already referred, that technological achievements presuppose the prior existence of valid knowledge. If this were true it would follow that the achievement of certain results would be evidence of an understanding of the process by which the results are achieved. Although it would by no means follow that science thus bolstered up by technology was capable of settling any and every question, there would nevertheless be some justification for the current "belief in science." So it is important that we should try to get to the bottom of the relation between knowledge and action. Let us start with a very simple, obvious case. We all eat and more or less successfully digest our food, but this does not mean that we understand the process of digestion, or that any pronouncements we may choose to make about the energy which is needed for the life of man and the nature of this energy must be valid. But this is precisely the way in which we tend to speak about what we call the practical achievements of science. We think that because some process has been successfully carried out, especially when it is done on a large scale, the phenomena involved are understood—at any rate by those who were, responsible for its first discovery. We then go on to think that, because the phenomena are understood, conclusions drawn from the explanations of the process have a special kind of validity. We term this "having been scientifically proved" or "established by science." Let us see how this inference applies to some well-known achievements of technology, which I have chosen quite at random.

We can start with the Industrial Revolution, that whole process which after the middle of the 18th century began to give mankind the ability to use energy on a much larger scale than in any previous known period. The primary cause was the burning of coal instead of wood. Everyone knows that during the 18th century a crisis threatened because there was not enough wood to make the iron that was needed; so we learned to burn coal instead. Although people began successfully to burn coal and thus changed the course of history, the most fantastic notions existed as to what happens when anything does burn. The phlogiston theory, which at that time was regarded as "valid scientific knowledge," is so absurd that we can only marvel today at the ingenuity with which the scientists twisted the facts to fit the theory. But all this absurdity did not stop the rapid growth in the use of coal and the consequent transformation of life in the Western world. It was not until the end of the 18th century, in 1783, that Lavoisier first presented a more reasonable picture of the combustion process in terms of the combination of the elements carbon, hydrogen and oxygen. Even to this day we cannot say with any confidence that we "know" the nature of a flame.

Or consider the steam engine. It was in the middle of the 1770s that James Watt produced a whole series of inventions connected with the steam engine which, second to the burning of coal, was the main factor in making the Industrial Revolution possible. At that time no one understood anything about the theory of the heat engine. It was not until much later, in 1824, that Sadi Carnot, a little-known, badly treated French teacher of mathematics, who died at the age of thirty six, produced a theory which gave some understanding of the motive power of steam and of the type of engine which is required for its efficient conversion. This happened sixty years after the steam engine had been invented by Watt, and at a time when people were already pointing to these extraordinary achievements as indications that man was gaining mastery over nature, and were taking for granted that something was understood and known about the process of gaining this "mastery".

A year or two before Carnot's treatise on the heat engine cycle, Michael Faraday published his famous researches on the connection between electricity and magnetism, researches which led to all the marvellous technological developments of electrical engineering which is a third great factor in changing the external life of man. The explanation Faraday himself employed for the purpose of reporting his researches was no more than a convenient fiction, useful only for the purpose of description. It was not until very much later—in 1897, when J. J. Thomson established the existence of the small particles now known as electrons—that something began to be understood about the nature of electricity. This happened seventy-five years after the practical discoveries of Faraday and after technological advances had already made electricity available for use on a large scale. Later still, the conception of the electron as a tiny compact particle was replaced by the notion of it as a wave, and there is no doubt that this notion in turn will be superseded by still other theories. Meanwhile the march of electrical technology goes forward, and if the average man thinks about it at all when he switches on the current he confidently assumes that the scientists who specialize in these matters know what electricity is.

The atomic theory in chemistry is often cited as an example of the possibility of doing things without knowing what is going on. During the greater part of the 19th century chemical science made extraordinary progress by the use of the conception of the atoms as permanent indestructible entities, identical with one another for each chemical element. The indestructibility of the atom was so widely assumed to be "scientifically proved" that it was taken into philosophical speculation and regarded as evidence in support of views on the nature of reality which had a profound effect upon beliefs concerning the nature and destiny of man. Later, when the theory of the indestructibility of the atom was exploded, the beliefs based upon it continued to remain current, and have contributed in no small measure to the confusion of present-day thought.

A striking example of the inference from knowing to doing is to be found in the rise of the so-called Theory of Evolution. Basing his argument very largely upon the successful achievements of mankind in the breeding of new varieties of animals and plants, Darwin concluded that a similar mechanism might be operative in the origin of new species. The success of this theory in giving a consistent account of the connection between living animals and plants and those whose skeletons are preserved, in the rocks, has led people to overlook the essential fact that nothing whatever was known of the mechanism by which the inner change required to produce a new species could be effected. The all-important distinction between a practical achievement—that is, the successful classification of biological data—and the understanding of a process or the way in which a species arose, is scarcely ever made. Here again the practical achievement is assumed to have validated the theory, and for the average person biological evolution by some kind of automatic mechanical process is assumed to be "scientifically proved". Although the rise of genetic science, the origin of which had no connection at all with the theory of Evolution, has given us some understanding of the process of breeding it has so far failed to disclose a mechanism convincing even to the biologists themselves of the manner in which the separation of two species incapable of interbreeding can come about. In spite of this, the concept of universal evolution as an automatic mechanical process is nowadays accepted almost without question and where it runs counter to theological or philosophical doctrines previously held, it is the latter which are abandoned or reconstructed in subservience to what is supposed to be "scientific truth".

A remarkable feature of the history of science is that, in spite of the obvious impermanence of all scientific theory, there is always a tendency to draw final conclusions affecting our attitude towards man and his place in the universe from the particular theories which happen to be fashionable at a given moment. Although scientists who think seriously about these matters know very well that a theory is only a convenient method of description and not a statement about fact, they are no less prone than others to condemn as unscientific any views which do not conform to the theories in vogue. I am convinced that this strange attitude of mind owes a great deal to the confusion between science and technology. That which is solidly established is the fact that this or that industry is operating on a very large scale. Scientific theory has much less to do with such achievements, than people imagine it to have. We can witness the spectacle of scientists tumbling over one another to produce theories rather than admit that some practical achievement has been realized not through knowledge but through a kind of feeling or sense for the way in which a natural process will operate. Many of the greatest scientists have been people impatient with theory: they have been led directly by this sensing of the process of nature, to carry out their experiments, and so have established some regularity or law which can be turned to practical account. Faraday was one such; Pasteur another; Rutherford a third. But the average layman tends to respect scientific theories, to attach some kind of validity to the theory itself, and in the outcome to equate theory with knowledge and, as a result, to cherish the belief that theories can be or have been "scientifically proved."

All this is very obvious to students of the history of philosophy and science: if this book were being written

for such students I should be wasting my time and theirs
in labouring the point. Unfortunately, those whose
business it is to know these things seldom recognise
that it is their duty to remove the general misunderstanding and to make clear to those who put their faith
in science that the scientific method is much more
limited in its application than they suppose it to be.

Before I leave this subject I should like to refer to
one example of the general unreliability of scientific
theory in a case where there is no supporting structure
of technological achievement. This is the origin of the
solar system. Children are taught at school that the
solar system originated from a swirling mass of incan-
descent gas which gradually cooled down and finally
solidified to produce the sun from which, in turn, the
planets were somehow thrown off in consequence of
the swirling motion. In other words, they are taught
some version of the Kant-Laplace theory, which is one
hundred and seventy years old and has been conclu-
sively demonstrated to be incapable of explaining
the observed distribution of momentum in the solar
system. Nevertheless, the belief that the sun and the
planets originated in some such way is almost univer-
sally held with a conviction no less firm than that
which supported our forefathers' belief in the Book of
Genesis. The origin of the solar system is a delicate
subject among astronomers today, for it exposes
more than anything else our complete ignorance of
celestial processes. All the theories which have been
invented are speculative and hazardous, designed if

possible to explain the observed facts in terms of some preconceived opinion about the way in which things might have happened. A conference was held in London not long ago to discuss theories of the origin of the solar system. Several such theories were put forward, each quite incompatible with all the others and each was strongly advocated by the particular school that happened to be working on it. But not one of these theories will account for even the known facts. So inexplicable, indeed, is the existence of the solar system, with its peculiar relationships of masses and momenta, that some astronomers have drawn the bizarre conclusion that our planetary system must be almost if not quite unique in the universe—an idea which at one time was misguidedly seized upon as sufficient justification for belief in the uniqueness of man as the sole rational creature on the sole habitable planet in the universe. Our very inability to account for the arising of the solar system should give pause to those who attempt to construct scientific cosmogonies based upon the assumption that no conscious agencies are involved.

Now I come to the main subject-matter of the present chapter: the rise and eventual dominance of theories based on the assumption that man has no better means of knowing reality than reliance upon his own experience and his own intellectual processes. It is the conquest of the belief in human reason over the belief in divine revelation. The belief that man has nothing better than himself and his own reason to rely upon merges insensibly into confidence that he can make a success of his, affairs; this in turn, when things go wrong, breaks down into the disease of "hoping for the best." Moreover, it is incompatible with the doctrine that we are not what we should be and that we have nothing in ourselves upon which we can rely until we create it by our own conscious labour and intentional suffering. Gurdjieff's doctrine is not irrational or anti-rational but it. does imply that the un- ~ developed, unpurified reason of people—especially after it has passed through the disastrous process of modern education—is hopelessly inadequate for a wise ordering of life. It was with this in mind that I took as the title of this chapter, "Science and Philosophy—the Fount of Unwisdom." In order to illustrate the pernicious influence of belief in science as a source of valid knowledge, I -am now going to consider three stages in the development of thought since the time of the early Greek philosophers. I have chosen these, not because they are uniquely important, but because they illustrate three great errors into which mankind has fallen.

Greek philosophy has always played and continues to play a dominating part in our thought. We have done very little in 2500 years except elaborate and embellish ideas derived from the Greek thinkers. I shall not go back to the origins of Greek philosophy but refer only to Aristotle, whose theories have left their mark on all our scientific thinking. Aristotle enjoyed for a very long time among Christian and Islamic peoples a prestige which can scarcely be exaggerated. We have to throw our minds back more than a thousand years to understand, the unquestioning acceptance of his theories by Christian and Moslem thinkers of almost every school. There have been times when he was regarded as a divinely inspired teacher and placed on so high a level that, even for Christian theologians, his authority was equal to that of the Fathers of the Church. Even now, when we have repudiated or left behind the details of almost everything he taught, the attitude of mind which he represents has become so fundamental to our way of thinking that we are scarcely capable of standing aside and criticizing its bases.

The attitude of mind crystallized in Aristotle's teaching has been particularly disastrous for all subsequent human thought. It is the notion that the human mind is capable of making ultimate judgments on the truth or falsity of propositions regarding the nature of reality. It is true that this idea did not originate with Aristotle but with the earlier Greek philosophers, but it was the Aristotelian logic (so-called) in which this notion was enshrined that fixed it in the minds of subsequent generations. Although the severe limitations of deductive logic are now fully recognized, the presupposition remains that anything that is true must be capable of being expressed and recognized as such in terms which the human mind can grasp. Scholastic philosophy imported this axiom into theological enquiry and the Middle Ages saw the strange spectacle of reverence for God displaying itself in the attempt to prove His existence by logical argument.

The persistence of the Aristotelian doctrines can be seen in the present-day demand that, to be acceptable, any doctrine must first be "scientifically proved."

The grotesqueness of the whole procedure should be evident to anyone with even an elemental notion of the working of the human brain, an instrument capable of only a peculiarly limited number of operations. It is fairly clear that it works almost exclusively by affirming or denying the truth of one out of two alternative possibilities presented to the momentary awareness present in the thinking brain. It can work only with words or symbols conveying meanings which must be very simple to be used at all. As soon as the inner content of a symbol passes beyond the capacity for immediate experience of the person who uses it, it becomes merely a sign with which he operates in a kind of mental void. To suppose that such an instrument is the highest possible mode of apprehending reality is a most hazardous and improbable speculation. It is infinitely more probable that Newton was right when, in speaking of one of the greatest achievements of the human intellect, he described himself as a child playing with pebbles on the seashore while the whole ocean of truth lay unexplored beyond him.

The second great disaster to Western philosophy came very much later, at the beginning of the 17th century, with Descartes, whose impact upon the thought of the world happened most unfortunately to coincide with a period of astonishing success of (as it is termed) physical science. Just as Aristotle was responsible for crystallizing and making permanent an earlier misconception of the supremacy of the human mind, so Descartes crystallized and made permanent an earlier misconception of the nature of reality. The misconception was the division of reality into thoughts and things, into thinking substance and extended substance. This dualism, which divides into mutually closed compartments the world of experience and the world of physical processes, has done more than anything else to destroy in people's minds the possibility of realizing the true nature of man. Descartes' conceptions are fundamentally anti-religious; but, owing partly to the great prestige he enjoyed through his mathematical discoveries and partly to his attitude of subservience towards the Church, his doctrines penetrated into religious thought. Their harmful character can be understood if we reflect upon Gurdjieff's teaching that man creates his soul by conscious labour and intentional suffering. According to the Cartesian dualism, body and soul must be incapable of effective mutual interaction. It is therefore meaningless to suggest that the labours and sufferings of the body can contribute directly to the growth of the soul. Conversely, the conception that by inner development a man can completely transform his power to act upon the external world is equally meaningless for any strict dualian. It so happens that Descartes himself was a very great physical scientist and lived at the beginning of a period when physical science achieved its most

notable successes in establishing the uniformity of
the processes which occur in all mechanical systems.
For the first time in Western thought a law had been
established which appeared to have universal validity,
extending not only throughout all terrestrial phenomena
but into the heavens as well. The achievements of
Eastern thinking were at that time unknown. It was
not realized, for example, that a far greater thinker,
Gotama Buddha, had established universal laws of even
more critical importance in his doctrines of universal
causality and universal decay. It was not realized that
still more significant laws affecting the very structure
of reality had been worked out in prehistoric China.
And, above all, it was not realized that in Asia unsuspected knowledge had long existed of the possibility
of developing in man powers com-pared with which
the operations of logical thinking are mere children's
toys. In the absence of all this knowledge, the discoveries of Descartes, Galileo and Newton and their
successors impressed contemporary Western humanity
scarcely less than did the achievements of Aristotle
and the Greek physical scientists 1700 years before.

The belief that mechanistic explanations of natural
processes are more logical and consistent than are
conceptions which take purpose into account, is only
one of the pernicious tendencies which have become
buried in scientific thought as a result of the Cartesian
philosophy. For the understanding of human nature, a
still more disastrous outcome was the identification of

the human being with his own thinking process. The realization that man possesses three spiritualised parts, each of which has to make a full contribution to a normally balanced existence, was established long before the rise of Greek philosophy. It can be found in the oldest Upanishads and in other early literature of the Aryan races. According to the psychological researches conducted by Gurdjieff and his fellow-workers, it was understood and made the basis of practical life in the Sumerian and Babylonian civilizations and in the lost civilizations of Central Asia. The tradition reached, and was to some extent understood by, Plato and his followers. Although distorted and seriously misunderstood by the early Christian Fathers, it entered into their early psychological teaching. It persisted in the West and found expression in Meister Eckhart and in various schools of thought which remained active up to the 17th century. From Descartes it received its death-blow. Since his time the thinking mind has been regarded as the one and only seat of human experience. Feeling and sensing have been taken either as subsidiary activities of the thinking mind or as purely physical processes occurring in the body. The Confusion between these two conceptions can be seen in Descartes' own treatment of the passions. Those who revolted against this distortion of the facts of experience—for example the English philosopher-psychologist John Locke—were misunderstood and misinterpreted. It was not until late in the 19th century that psychology again recognized the existence of processes which although they do not take place in the thinking mind nevertheless have a profound influence upon human behaviour. Even so, the influence of Cartesian thought has remained so strong that the data which forced the recognition of hon-mental processes were not interpreted, as they should have been, in terms of the three spiritualised or potentially conscious parts of the human psyche.

There is one further consequence of the Cartesian division of reality into the two categories of thinking substance and extended substance which makes it difficult for contemporary people to understand the teaching of Gurdjieff. The only way in which the contradictions of -a dualistic metaphysics can be removed is to recognise that matter and experience are two aspects of the same reality. This view has been put forward by many philosophers, notably by Whitehead, but no one has been able to make the necessary step towards realizing that matter-experience is of different orders. It was dimly understood by McTaggart in his *Nature of Existence,* but his idealistic predispositions prevented him from seeing how it could be expressed in a concrete form. It emerges naturally from the conception of eternity regarding which I made a few preliminary suggestions in *The Crisis in Human Affairs.* It is fully expressed, and its significance for a right understanding of man and his place in the Universe is made clear, in Gurdjieff's own writings.

Enough has been said to show why I described the

influence of Descartes as a major disaster in western thought. He chiefly was responsible for the prevalence of dualistic theories which prevent people from understanding the possibility that man is a being destined for self-creation. He contributed largely to the belief that mechanistic or causal explanations should be adopted in preference to those which invoke an end or purpose. He placed obstacles in the way of understanding that man is a three-brained being. He contributed not a little to our inability to see that the self or "I" in man does not arise automatically but has to be brought into existence by intentional work. Although nominally a Christian and even painfully subservient to the Church—witness his refusal to meet Galileo when he visited Italy— his philosophy was incompatible with any genuine religious feeling and his influence has greatly contributed to the rise of atheism in scientific thought.

It has been suggested that Cartesian dualism is not incompatible with a noble view of human destiny. Man is represented as a two-natured being; fated over the ages gradually to emancipate himself from gross "matter" and exist more and more as "spirit"; until, ultimately, matter will be shed as a worn-Out garment and the human spirit will rejoice in the sunshine of the Divine Spirit.

Such doctrines, to my understanding, founder on the rock of psycho-somatic interaction. If spirit and matter act on one another they must have some common property which makes spirit material and matter spiritual. Once this is admitted (and it seems inevitable unless we are prepared to accept some doctrine of "pre-established" harmony) "matter" and "spirit" become merely names for different grades of the same primordial substance.

Moreover, for me there is something more convincing and more splendid in the conception of redemption of the physical world by conscious labour from the degenerative influence, of time than in that of escape from a material world condemned to inevitable destruction. Gurdjieff's doctrine of the three modes of Being makes dualism unnecessary, and I believe that no one, if he could avoid doing so, would wish to flounder in its morass of unresolved contradiction.

The third disaster, which occurred about two hundred years later, was the entry into scientific thinking and so into the general thought processes of contemporary people, of the doctrine of Evolution conceived as necessary automatic progress in an upward direction. It often has been pointed out that the idea of progress is a relatively new factor in human thought. By the Greeks the historical process was> conceived as a series of cycles in which similar situations recurred. There was also present the idea of an earlier Golden Age from which there had been a progressive deterioration. To the early Christians also—and the concept was derived not from Greek but from Jewish thought—the world presented itself as in a deteriorating situation, which inevitably would end

in final disaster and be followed by a sudden transformation into the world of the Resurrection. It goes
without saying that the notion of automatic progress
has been quite absent from Oriental thought.

Even to the 18th-century reformers, hope for the
future did not present itself in terms of automatic
progress but rather in those of the destruction of
tyranny and the return of mankind to a normal state of
existence conceived as corresponding to his own intrin-
sically good social nature.

Were the emergence into human thought of the idea
of progress to be associated with any single name, it
would probably be that of the German philosopher
Hegel, with his doctrine of the Dialectic of the Notion.
Hegel, of course, was fully imbued with the Aristotelian notion of the supremacy of reason: in fact, he
regarded reason as the fundamental law of nature by
which alone man and the universe were brought into
harmony. Starting from a primitive condition of undifferentiated being, the law of reason was presumed
to operate with the passage of time so as to bring
about progressively higher and more spiritual modes
of being culminating finally in the conquest of the pure
notion. It is not easy today to recapture the prestige
which THE SYSTEM (it must be written with capital
letters) enjoyed at the beginning of the 19th century.
In a world of obvious suffering and injustice the
historical, absurdity of Hegel's contention that the
millennium had already been reached, was primarily
responsible for the collapse of his doctrine. The idea

of necessary progress by the same mechanism but interpreted in materialistic instead of spiritual terms was
seized upon by Engels and Marx and made the foundation of their doctrine of class warfare and the necessary
emergence of yet another millennium from which
injustice and suffering would be banished. By a historical accident the publication of *Das Kapital* almost
coincided in date with the publication of Darwin's
Origin of Species which appeared to provide "scientific proof" of the validity of the doctrine of necessary
automatic progress.

Once again a theory claiming scientific validity had
arisen which was to have pernicious consequences
for succeeding generations. I have already referred
to the distinction which should be drawn between the
practical value of the theory of Evolution as a means of
classifying biological data and the danger of assuming
that the mechanism of Evolution is understood. That
there has been an evolution of biological forms at least
within individual species can be regarded as established as against any doctrine of a finished ^creation.
It is quite another thing to assert that this evolution
can be explained in terms of blind accidental processes
operating without any purpose and devoid of any kind
of conscious guidance or direction. The expectation
of a millennium as the outcome of the blind conflict
of class warfare has been falsified as completely as
the Hegelian belief that a perfect form of state was
emerging in the German Principalities.

We take for granted that we are better than our

ancestors and that our modes of life are superior to theirs. In support of this belief we recklessly distort the evidence and disregard those facts which cannot be explained. It is assumed, for example, that our science and our technology are in every respect an advance upon anything which existed in the remote past. If this were true it would be difficult to account for some of the achievements of prehistoric man, such as the domestication of animals and plants. At some time in the early history of mankind this extraordinary technological achievement was realized. We depend very largely for our existence upon agricultural achievements the origin of which goes back beyond the dawn of history. With all the progress of biological science we have scarcely succeeded in domesticating a single animal of a single plant not known to our early ancestors. It is true that through breeding we have made great improvements, but all our accomplishments in this respect are not impressive when compared with those of what we are pleased to call "primitive" man. There is another technical achievement of the past of which we have actually proved ourselves incapable today. This is the creation of a new linguistic form. The failure of the various attempts, which have been made to create a new universal language must convince anyone capable of impartial thought that a high level of accomplishment stands to the credit of those unknown forbears who between 10,000 and 20,000 years ago discovered the means of adapting abstract symbols to the thought processes of the human mind. It is only from willful prejudice that we can assert that these things were done by ignorant savages working by a blind process of trial and error—or any other automatic unconscious process.

One unfortunate consequence of the doctrine of automatic blind evolution is that it prevents us from perceiving that a genuine, but quite different, evolutionary process can really occur. Development from a lower form of existence to a higher is possible, although only as a result of conscious, purposive action. It is at this point that the full incompatibility of Gurdjieff's teaching with the whole of science and philosophy since Greek times can be understood. Going against the teaching of Aristotle he denies the supremacy of the human mind and its capacity for knowing; he asserts instead that it is a limited instrument which must be developed by conscious work before it can be credited with the possession of objective reason. He denies the Cartesian dualism of thinking and extended substance and asserts instead a hierarchy of matter and experience in which man occupies a very low place in his natural undeveloped state, but which he can ascend stage by stage to a degree of development which will make him significant not only for his immediate. environment hut also for cosmic purposes of a very high order. As against the automatic necessary evolution of Hegel, Marx and Darwin he asserts that all progress in the upward direction must be purposive and can be achieved only through conscious labour and intention-al suffering. I have already referred to the distinction he makes between three Modes of Existence. When once the significance of this distinction is sufficiently grasped it becomes obvious that western science and philosophy, though possessing the very keys of a right understanding, have been led astray through failure to grasp one fundamental principle, the principle that, in order to *know* it is necessary to *be*.

CHAPTER IV

THE TRAGEDY OF CONTEMPORARY RELIGION

AMONG the many strange things taught to children in their geography lessons are statistics of the world's population distributed into various racial, economic and cultural groups. On one page of the atlas you find a map of the world showing the distribution of the various religions, and statistics indicating how many Buddhists, Christians, Hindus, Moslems and the rest are living in the world. The numbers total something over two thousand million—the estimated total population of the world—and the child, if he thinks about it at all, naturally concludes that every living human being is either a Buddhist, a Christian or a Moslem, and so on up to the number of religious groups adopted. Sometimes, it is true, there is a remainder: for example, in the atlas at which I just happened to look, the division is into Christians, Mohammedans, Confucians and Buddhists, Brahmans and Heathens—the last-mentioned shown mostly as inhabiting Africa and regions near the Arctic Circle and mercifully comprising not more than a few per cent of the world's population! Now if the child were to speculate—as indeed children do—sitting before his atlas and gazing at the regions marked with non-heathen colours, he might be led to experience a sense of relief that God occupies so great a place in the life of man. He would probably find it difficult to reinforce this feeling by observing the lives of the grown-up people with whom he was in contact and might begin to develop an incredulity which would extend even to other lessons of geography.

We know only too well that these divisions mean very little indeed in regard to the inner convictions and beliefs, the way of life and the dominating motives, of the people concerned. At the same time, we do associate with the term, religion; some conception and some beliefs and a way of life. Unless it means at least this, religion means nothing at all. Most people have some idea (though often it is extraordinarily wide of the truth) of what is taught by the different religions about man and his destiny and the way he should behave. Let us begin by asking ourselves in the simplest terms how far the lives of various great communities correspond to anything which is prescribed in the religious beliefs they are assumed to hold. According to most recent statistics, the Buddhist religion with its various deriva-tives has the greatest number of followers. We must not place too much reliance upon such figures: those who prepare them usually have very little knowledge of the content of religious teaching and rely upon names or verbal descriptions given by others almost as ignorant as themselves. We can say, however, that there are great regions of the world where the Buddhist tradition dominates whatever exists of religious life. Now, respect for living creatures and abstention from violence in any form has always been a feature of the Buddhist tradition, and for a long period of time it operated to diminish the incidence of war and almost entirely brought to an end wars of conquest. That the horror of war was something very real to the ancient Buddhist can be seen from the Rock Edicts of King Asoka in India and the results of the labours of the first Buddhist missionaries in China. What is the situation today? It is mainly among peoples shown on the maps as predominantly Buddhist that this particular scourge of mankind is now in progress. More than half the "Buddhists" are engaged in some form of war or civil strife.

Or we may look at the lives of individuals. It was a central part, perhaps the very essence, of the teaching of Gotama Buddha to his immediate disciples that it is only by his own personal striving that a man can be liberated from the endless suffering of corporeal existence. Marga, the Way, with its eight-fold striving, was the. only means of removing those inherent, defects which prevent man from attaining liberation; According to one of. the oldest traditions the last words of the dying Gotama Buddha were: "Work out your own salvation with diligence." Opposed to all forms of external ritual, he particularly condemned sacrifices or ritual offerings because they distracted man from the realization that everything depended upon his own inner work. Yet today one

sees everywhere in Buddhist countries temples with
elaborate rituals, priests assuming that very role of
intermediary between man and the higher powers which
the Founder of their religion had condemned in the
Brahmins who were his contemporaries. The strenuous
work of inner collectedness indicated by the Pali
word, sati-sampajja, which calls upon every Buddhist
to practice constantly the state of being mindful and
self-possessed, has taken the ingenious form of prayer
wheels kept in motion by a flick of the fingers. And
even this has proved too much! There are prayer-wheels
driven by the wind; and recently even the resources of
western technology have been brought to, bear in the
introduction of prayer-wheels which can be installed and
permanently worked by electric motors. I do not deny
that there are many thousands of devout Buddhists, but
for the main part even these entertain beliefs of a kind
explicitly repudiated in the most authentic records of
the personal teaching of Gotama. Gotama is represented in almost all records as deriding all speculation over
ultimate human destiny. He taught that it was useless to
ask whether or not a man existed after death, whether
or not his personality survived in some form, whether
the enlightened beings who do become Arahants can
be said either to have or not to have existence in space
and time. None of these things could be understood
except by those who were already enlightened and,
for the rest, it was necessary simply to persevere with
the duties of the Way. Today Buddhism is as full of

doctrines about heaven and hell and of elaborate theories concerning the future life as is any other religion.

In India Buddhism was supplanted nearly two thousand years ago by Hinduism with the recovery of the hereditary Brahmin priesthood. Brahminism in its purest form is founded upon a very simple and noble teaching that man (purusha) is made in the image of his Creator (Purusha), and that his highest welfare consists in divesting himself of the illusion of his separate individuality in order to realize for himself the ultimate truth that Atman is Brahman. There was a time, only a few centuries ago, when Hinduism was a living force for a great number of people existing in appalling conditions of oppression in India under the rule of the Mogul invaders. Out of this oppression and suffering was distilled a very noble way of life. Teachers of this way of life were respected as truly great men although they enjoyed neither ecclesiastical authority nor political power. But what is Hinduism today? It has become simply a political label. To be a Hindu is to be in antagonism to non-Hindus and, particularly, to Christians and Moslems. Very little remains of anything resembling a religious way of life. The simplicity of the primitive doctrine has been overlaid with elaborate beliefs in gods identified with the possession of special human virtues or even physical powers and political attributes. In the Tantric schools there is certainly much valuable and authentic knowledge with regard to man and the methods whereby his latent powers can be developed. There are also undoubtedly genuine schools in which practical knowledge of these methods has been preserved European travelers, without much difficulty, can come in contact with certain of these schools and can meet individual teachers who exercise a great influence upon a small personal environment. But for the great masses of the Hindu population religion has become a means through which their suggestibility is exploited for political purposes. A strange hotchpotch of Eastern and Western ideas has taken possession of the "intelligentsia," for whom religion has little to do with either inner belief or an outward way of life.

Islam, the next of the great religions, has achieved its present great extension only within the last thousand years. This is no doubt one reason why it has, on the whole, departed less from the teachings of its Founder than have the other great religions of the world from theirs. His teachings, moreover, are contained in records of a high degree of authenticity: The Koran and the Hadissat. Probably it is due most of all to the practical wisdom of Mohammed that his followers in many countries still practice almost unchanged the methods of self-discipline which he prescribed in the form of the Namaz, the five-fold daily canonical prayer preserved from degenerating into the mumbling of a formula by the postures and bodily movements enjoined. The annual Ramazan, the month of fasting, is devised in such a way as to provide a practical task of a simple character. The

same applies to the Hajj, the obligation to make once in
a lifetime the pilgrimage to the Holy Places. The effect
of these precautions is to make it difficult for a man to
describe himself as a Moslem without doing at any rate
something about his external life. Moreover, in many
Moslem countries the codes of ordinary behaviour,
derived mainly from the Hadissat, have been taken as
the basis of political jurisprudence and the Sheri'i law
has maintained a link between religious and civil life
which has disappeared in most other parts of the world.

Notwithstanding the relatively simple practical
demands made upon a Moslem believer, these have
proved too much for most Islamic communities,
especially those which have come in close contact
with Western influence. With the strange propensity of
human beings for turning good institutions into means
of producing harmful results, the very identification of
civil and religious life has tended towards a degeneration of the Islamic faith into political fanaticism. In
many parts of the world to be a Moslem is to carry
a political label. It is not very long since Pan-Isla-
mism threatened to become a serious political factor
in the affairs of the world; but when put to the test it
became evident that the fire of religious conviction had
burned so low that very few Moslems were prepared
to make any personal sacrifice for the attainment of
their declared ideals. The creed of Islam has become
a matter of talk—more correctly, perhaps, a matter of
shouting; and but very little more.

It would be entirely wrong to suggest that there are not in every Mohammedan country many devout Moslems who live by the simple creed that man exists to serve God and to break down the barriers which his own defects and weaknesses have built between himself and his Creator. I have met many Moslems the simplicity of whose conversation and the seemliness of whose lives have made them an example to us all. There are also profounder traditions, of which Sufism is the best known, in which is preserved knowledge of ancient methods for the development of the latent powers in man. Until recent times many of these were widely practiced by Dervishes, sometimes living in communities and sometimes withdrawn from the world into solitary places. Under the Ottoman Empire the Dervishes were greatly respected and their brotherhoods, to which members of the Imperial family were proud to belong, exercised a great influence and that almost without any political taint. One of the decisive consequences of the downfall of the Ottoman Empire was the dissolution of the Dervish communities in Turkey and the campaign of misrepresentation and slander against their way of life, a campaign undertaken with the avowed objective of "modernizing" the Turkish people. The knowledge of practical methods for helping the work of self-creation through "conscious labour and intentional suffering," possessed by various Dervish brotherhoods has not been entirely lost, but it has become increasingly difficult of access. This is a great misfortune, since such knowledge contains more of practical value than does that of the better known mystical schools of India. Whereas, even during my stay in Turkey only thirty years ago, much could be learned about the work of the Dervishes, and they were treated with great respect, in the comparatively short intervening period things have so changed that it is now a political if not a criminal offence to belong to a Dervish community or even to speak of them in public. This is a measure of the rapidity with which the sense of the reality of the religious life is disappearing from former Moslem countries.

From the teachings of Moses and the Jewish prophets have come some of the fundamental religious conceptions of nearly half the world: for example, Monotheism and the belief in Sacred Individuals sent from or designated by God to mediate between God and man. Also, certain rules of conduct prescribed in the Mosaic Law are common to Jews, Moslems and Christians alike. But there remain only a few million people, and those mostly belonging to one race, who profess to adhere to the original Mosaic tradition; even among Jews, for the great majority, the religion of Moses has ceased to enter effectively into either their inner beliefs or their external lives. As with Hinduism or Islam, Judaism as a religion has given place to a political creed. (It has been said that the Jews are now divided into three categories: Judaists, Zionists and Jews who are neither the one nor the other.) As in all other communities, so among the

Jews are there devout adherents of Judaism whose lives are regulated by the elaborate code of behaviour prescribed in the Mosaic Law and the Talmud, whose faith is in the God of their Fathers and whose hope is in the fulfilment of His will. There are, too, Rabbis who still preserve ancient traditional knowledge transmitted from generation to generation; but they grow fewer and are hard to meet. Even those admirable Jewish qualities of united and harmonious family life and fortitude in persecution, have weakened, and the spiritual force of Judaism has been swallowed up in political ambitions and in purposes sometimes even less worthy of admiration.

To complete the story, we must turn our attention to Christianity. It holds up to our view the saddest picture of all. On the map of the world many areas bear the colour which stands for a Christian people. The makers of these maps —presumably not knowing what else to do—still paint this colour over countries where the repudiation of all religion is written into the constitution of the State and where branches of an organization bearing the quaint title, "Society of the Ungodly," are recognized channels of official propaganda. The history of Christianity in Soviet Russia since the October Revolution has been one of simple political expediency. At one time during the 1939-45 war it suddenly transpired that religious exhortation was an aid to military morale. At another period "toleration" (as it was termed) of religious communities appeared to provide an equally good weapon

of propaganda in foreign countries. We can easily
become indignant at such treatment of, and such an
attitude towards, the religious life; but in what sense
can any "Christian" country assert that it is Christian
in anything but name? How small a part does anything
that could be called Christian teaching play in the way
of life, in the dominating motives and in the beliefs of
the majority of people who are described as Christians?
In respect of these three things, the teaching of Jesus
Christ was unequivocal. He preached the doctrine of
the Kingdom and asserted that, unless the search for
the Kingdom was the dominating motive in the life
of a man, he and all his works would inevitably be
destroyed. He also prescribed the way of life through
which alone the Kingdom of Heaven could be attained.
Whatever differences of doctrine or opinion may exist
among the many conflicting Christian sects, none can
deny these sayings without impugning the authenticity
of the only reliable records of that which Jesus Christ
himself taught to his immediate disciples. And in no
other of the religions of the world have the injunctions
of the Founder been so completely disregarded.

The sacredness of human life and the abhorrence of
violence, carried to the extreme limit in the passage
beginning: "But I say unto you, that ye resist not evil,"
was so consistently expressed in the words of Jesus that
no possible distortion could bring them into harmony
with the approval of war in any form. It is most
probable that the immediate cause of the Crucifixion

was the refusal of Jesus to sanction even the appearance of consent to the Messianic insurrection against the Romans of his day. Yet the whole history of the Christian peoples has been a history of war, conquest, oppression and violence. The very event by which Christianity in 312a.d. became a world force—its adoption as the official religion of the Roman Empire—was a battle in which the words εν τουτω νικα were taken as a sign to encourage the Roman troops to ruthless massacre. The American continent, the largest single area in the world painted with the colour of Christianity, became Christian through wars of conquest and extermination the horror of which has no parallel in all recorded history. We have perhaps to some extent outgrown the habit of dividing mankind into Christians and heathens and regarding the Christian world as altogether (or at least fundamentally) good and the heathen world as altogether (or at least fundamentally) bad; but we still find it possible to assume a strange smug self-satisfaction about the superiority of the Christian tradition and "the Christian way of life" as compared with any other.

When living, among peoples of other religions I have not observed the same attitude on their part towards us, but rather one of surprise, not untinged with pity, that we should be so little able to see ourselves as we really are. When one succeeds in talking sincerely with Asiatic peoples one does not find so much a feeling of superiority as an inability to understand how, it can be that Christians can regard their religion as having a superior value or as being capable of establishing a good way of life. They point to the history of the Christian world, and ask us to explain the succession of wars and revolutions, the ruthless destruction and callous cruelty, which have been far more prevalent in Christendom than in any other part of the world. Many of them have read the Christian Gospels and have admired the sublime passages in which Christ says "Blessed are the peacemakers;" "Love your enemies;" and they ask how it can be that the Western peoples can presume to call themselves Christian. They have a sense of surprise and pity in regarding our failures but they cannot hide the disgust provoked by our hypocrisy. The miserable argument that Christianity could not be introduced except by conquest is countered by the example of the Buddhist missionaries who converted Tibet and China with no weapon but the power of their ideas. The argument that we were all savages once and that the evils of the past should be forgotten in the glories of the present, carries little conviction to peaceful peoples who have just seen the Christian nations emerging from two of the most ferocious wars of history only to prepare themselves to engage in a third.

The period of wars of conquest and religious persecution seems to be conveniently distant, and if things are not well with us today we can console ourselves with the thought that it is due to the weakening of religious feeling and that a religious revival would bring, us back to a better way of life. How little substance there is in any such hope can be seen if we cast our minds back to the period when religious revivals were the order of the day. This happens to coincide with the Industrial Revolution (1750-1850), a period to which any people and any race should look back with shame. During this period there proceeded, side by side, vehement proclamations of Christian doctrines as a revolt against the libertinism of the previous century, and the ruthless enslavement of people of the same race and creed as the oppressors. The very people who trampled underfoot every precept of the teaching of Jesus were very often reformers in their outward profession of a Christian life. The very man who prayed and read the Bible before his family and servants would hurry to his factory, manned by sweated—and often child—labour, with no thought but of the exercise of power and the amassing of wealth. The final overthrow of these iniquities came very largely not from the work of Christian reformers but from the struggles of men and women who were themselves in revolt against the Christian institutions. So low has the Christian teaching fallen in the eyes of many that the view has come to be widely held that progress towards greater tolerance and better relations between peoples depends upon the final "liquidation" of religious superstition. And this active hostility towards religion is a new phenomenon which has made its appearance almost exclusively in the countries which call themselves Christian.

It may be objected that I have attacked a Christendom

which does not exist; that no one takes seriously the assertion that the whole population of "Christian" countries is in any real sense Christian; that we should look to the devout and practicing members of the Christian churches in order to judge the true position of the Christian faith. The very fact that the word, churches, must be used in the plural is sufficient to remind us that devout and practicing Christians are not united among themselves and that the injunction, "Love one another," has long since been swallowed up in the *odium theologicum.* But even this may seem to mock unfairly at many thousands of people who are honestly trying to live a Christian life according to the particular form of institutional Christianity with which they happen to be associated. But we are entitled to ask one crucial question: "How far do the churches practice or even preach the teachings of Jesus Christ?" Almost everyone is neglected and replaced by conceptions which originated either in Greek philosophy or in the subsequent non-religious thought of the philosophers about whom I wrote in the preceding chapter.

Here I must revert to one decisive issue, to which I have referred several times: this is, the attitude of the Christian churches towards war. We all know how, within our own memory, virtually no outcry was heard from any of the Christian churches against all the horrors of the war which has only recently ended. Atrocities were perpetrated without condemnation almost equally by both sides. Perhaps the culmination of all the horror was the destruction by atom bombs of tens of thousands of quite helpless women and children in Japan. With the exception of those relatively small sects which have made the condemnation of violence a central feature of-their teaching, how few and how feeble were the voices of any Christians, ecclesiastics or laymen, raised even against "reprisals" and unnecessary destruction, let alone the whole process of war itself. From how many pulpits today can we hear a sermon preached on the text, "Resist not evil: but whosoever shall smite thee on thy right cheek, turn to him the other also"?

Those who take note of all these things tend often to speak about "the failure of religion," with the implication that Religion "ought" to "succeed." People can be heard to say: "If this is all that religion has done for mankind, we are better without it." Others say: "No, there is no hope unless we find a way of making religion a success."

The word, religion, is referred to as though it implied some kind of undertaking to be judged in terms of success or failure, and thus the notion is externalized and made to stand apart from man so that he can express opinions about it and judge it. It takes for granted that there is a something to which the word, religion, refers, and that this something can be good or bad, right or wrong, successful or unsuccessful, and so on. So strongly entrenched is this habit of thought that the reader will probably wonder what I am driving at, and think with impatience that in a serious situation I am splitting hairs about words; but it so happens that a very serious misunderstanding has entered and been perpetuated in our thinking by the use of the word, religion. I have myself used it throughout this chapter mainly in order to show the contradiction to which it leads. When we try to put our finger on religion, we find nothing but a mass of unrealities; yet we are forced to recognise that there is something very important and very necessary for the life of man hidden somewhere in the experience and the lives of people who have followed the religious way.

It seems to me that one cause of confusion is the word *religion* itself. This is essentially a pagan word. It appeared in the Latin language, long before the rise of Christianity, to denote a particular department of human activity—namely, that concerned with the affairs of the gods. For the early Romans religion in this sense was by no means the centre of man's life, and it was with no feeling of impiety or neglect of duty that the deep pondering on divine affairs of which Cicero spoke was left to the specialists, while the Roman citizen, whether of the aristocracy or of the plebs, was content to perform certain minimal duties required by custom. The conception of religion as a department of life remained even when Christianity had conquered the Roman Empire Greek thought did not separate art, religion and philosophy, or the pursuit of beauty, goodness and truth, into independent departments of human striving; but this division, for various reasons which it would take too long to discuss here, gradually acquired authority and has become established in modern times. The significant result is to place religious activity on a more or less equal footing with other activities of man, in direct conflict with the teaching of the Founders of every great religion.

It is noteworthy that in the Gospels the word, religion, does not once occur. Twice in the Acts and once in the Epistles we find the word θρησκεία which is translated "religion"; but it is not really equivalent to the word, religion; it means rather adoration or worship. No word equivalent to religion is used in connection with any other teaching. It is one of our habits in translating languages very different from, our own to use, false equivalents without realizing the misunderstandings which result. It is usual, for example, to translate the Sanskrit word, Dharma, and the Pali, Dhamma, as "religion", whereas they mean only "system" or "method." The Buddhist confession: "I put my faith in the Buddha, I put my faith in the Dharma, I put my faith in the Sangha," is not a declaration of faith in a religious teaching but in the efficacy of the methods belonging to the Way taught by Gotama. The Arabic word, Din, is usually translated "religion," but it is connected more closely with the idea of reckoning or judgment. Nearer to our use of "religion" is the word, Islam, which means salvation.

The concern of the Founders of the great religions

was not to offer man something external to himself, a body of doctrine, an institution, a "something" to occupy a certain place in his life, to safeguard him from particular dangers and to assure him particular benefits; it was to set him upon the *way*, the way of salvation, the way of the Kingdom. There was nothing remote or complicated in their teaching. "For this commandment which I command thee this day, it is not hidden from thee, neither is it far off. It is not in heaven, that thou shouldest say, Who shall go up for us to heaven, and bring it unto us, that we may hear it, and do it? Neither is it beyond the sea, that thou shouldest say, Who shall go over the sea for us, and bring it unto us, that we may hear it, and do it? But the word is very nigh unto thee, in thy mouth, and in thy heart, that thou mayest do it. See, I have set before thee this day life and good, and death and evil; In that I command thee this day to love the Lord thy God, to walk in his ways, and to keep his commandments and his statutes and his judgments, that thou mayest live and multiply: and the Lord thy God shall bless thee in the land whither, thou goest to possess it."* It is an invariable characteristic of the authentic teaching of the Founders that they rejected all theological speculation and ethical theory and emphasized the fundamental principle of self-perfecting through conscious labour and intentional suffering. It is far easier to speculate about the Nature of God than to struggle with one's own defects and to formulate rules

* Deuteronomy 30:11-16

of conduct than to live by the dictates of conscience. But whereas the consciousness of struggle can be shared by men and women of every race and creed, theological dogmas and ethical systems are among the most prolific sources of misunderstanding and conflict.

To understand the descent from practice to theory we may consider a typical sequence of events in the development of a religion. There is, first of all, the simple practical teaching of the Founder, free from philosophy or theological speculation. Then legends grow up which place the events in the life and death of the Founder in a false human perspective. This in turn leads to false expectations, disillusion and a reaction towards philosophy and speculative theology as a means of giving a new sanction to the growing organization of the future church. Then comes the conquest of the world—as Buddhism conquered with Asoka and Christianity with Constantine. The price of conquest is the surrender of all contact with the teaching of the Founder and the substitution of compromise doctrines—very often fantastically based on ephemeral notions of man and the universe which must ultimately be discredited. Finally, we have the spectacle of religious dogmas—even within the bosom of adherents of the same great religion—utterly in conflict and contradicting one another. Thus religion falls into disrepute and with it comes the loss of all power to help mankind. If, however, we think in terms of the practical injunctions given by the religious Founders to their immediate disciples, an almost complete identity of teaching becomes apparent. *Man is not what he should be.* His life has neither meaning nor value if it is interpreted solely in terms of his present existence. He must look beyond; but that he cannot do alone, for he is blind and his eyes must be opened. He must change his own being; but in order to do so he must pay the price, which is the sacrifice of the transient and illusory in order to gain the eternal and real. He must be born again; but before there can be resurrection, there must first be death. He must die to what he is, in order to become what he might be. Although he could do nothing without the help of the Sacred Individuals who prepare the way which he must follow, his destiny remains in his own hands, for it is his own labours and sacrifices that determine whether or not he, will justify his election. Moreover, in all this he does not ask for his own salvation alone, but must accept the utmost responsibility for the salvation of his neighbour. Throughout all, runs the thread that these things alone matter and without them life is an empty mockery.

I have chosen to formulate these principles in terms which approximate closely to those used by Gurdjieff in his writings, but I think there is no difficulty in recognizing a substantial identity of content with the most authentic records which have been transmitted to us of the direct teachings of the Sacred Individuals to their own immediate disciples. Divergences begin to appear only when we enter the field of subsequent theological speculation. I shall try by a few

examples to show that this is true for the teaching of
Jesus. I am not concerned with the events in the life of
Jesus of which the Gospel record is evidently misleading and incomplete, but with His recorded sayings,
many of which are unmistakably authentic. If we read
the Gospels attentively with the one aim of bringing
ourselves as far as is possible in contact with what Jesus
actually said and taught, certain convictions begin to
form in our minds about what, from any standpoint,
must be a genuine record.

The first of these is the preaching of the Kingdom
and the assertion that the attainment of the Kingdom is
the sole valid purpose of human life. Secondly, we have
the insistence that the attainment of the Kingdom is
difficult and is reserved for a few only. It is so difficult,
in fact, that again and again the disciples are represented as being astonished, and asking; "Who, then, shall be
saved?" We cannot fail to be impressed by the austerity
of the doctrine and the absence of the sentimental
optimism which gradually took possession of Christian
thought. Success and failure in the way are equally real.
Success is only for those who leave all and follow Him.
To fail is to perish. Although everything is promised
to those who surrender themselves entirely, there is no
suggestion of a loving hand to succour the unwilling
or fainthearted. Those who give all have nothing to
fear, but those who hold back, even for the sake of
performing what seem to be natural and obvious duties,
are rejected. The extreme form of this statement is:

"If any man come to me and hate not his father, and mother, and wife, and children, and brethren, and sisters, yes, and his own life also, he cannot be my disciple. And whosoever doth not bear his cross, and come after me, cannot be my disciple." Even if we regard this as a characteristic extravagance of the literary style of the writer of the third gospel, we find almost equivalent sayings in the more sober records of the first and second. Moreover, the doctrine of election is not, for Jesus, a guarantee of salvation. "Many are called, but few are chosen." Even the elect must earn their salvation; and there are also strong indications of teaching that salvation was possible even outside the circle of the elect: "And I say unto you, that many shall come from the east and west, and shall sit down with Abraham, and Isaac, and Jacob, in the kingdom of heaven. But the children of the kingdom shall be cast out into outer darkness; there shall be weeping and gnashing of teeth." In order to be saved a man must acquire something which he does not possess by nature. This is illustrated by the parable of the talents, and it leads to a saying which appears almost more often than any other in the three Synoptic Gospels: "For whosoever hath, to him shall be given, and he shall have more abundance; but whosoever hath not, from him shall be taken away even that he hath." Man is the servant of God, and his service is towards a hard master who reaps where he has not sown and gathers where he has not strawed. In these sayings we cannot fail to recognise an identity of content with the doctrine (adumbrated in the first chapter) of man created for a special cosmic purpose which can be accomplished only by the fact of his being free. He is given life and the possibility of creating for himself with that life an immortal soul. If he gains this soul, he has gained much more besides. If he does not create it even that which he hath—that is, his life—is taken away from him. The same is exemplified in the parable of the man without a wedding garment.

Finally, I need hardly remind the reader that throughout the Gospels runs the thread of conscious labour and intentional suffering as the price of eternal life.

If now we ask ourselves what is Christianity: is it the teaching of Jesus as recorded in these sayings; or is it the teaching of institutional Christianity as it exists at the present day; how should we answer? If we say it is the latter, we set the speculations of obviously fallible human thinkers above the words of Him whom every Christian must regard as a Sacred Individual, sent from Above. We cannot take refuge in the argument that the Gospel teaching is obscure and mysterious beyond the apprehension of ordinary people, requiring the interpretation of inspired theologians. There is nothing obscure or mysterious about the passages I have quoted. The only difficulty for us in accepting them is that they make demands which seem to be beyond our powers. Is it not at least possible that this may be because we have not seriously tried?

However it may be, we have to recognise that, during

nearly two thousand years only the fewest of the few have tried seriously to carry out Christ's teaching without reservation. But among these few we have authentic records of glorious successes. What has been the result of the turning away of the Christian world from the uncompromising teachings of the Founder? We have put in their place a great deal of sentimental nonsense, much of which is based on an obvious misinterpretation of the doctrine of vicarious atonement which makes it appear that salvation is for the many and damnation only for the few. The result has been that "Christians" have ceased to feel the necessity for work upon themselves. On the whole, the same can be said (as I tried to show at the beginning of this chapter) of the failures of the other great religions; so that throughout the world there has been a virtual disappearance of that intensive inner effort which is required for the work of self-creation.

At this point I can resume the exposition of Gurdjieff's teaching. According to this, the failure to perform the duty of conscious labour and intentional suffering shows itself not only in the destruction of the individual but also in disasters for the human race as a whole. People can never understand one another nor live in harmony together unless they are all striving for the aim of self-perfection. Conversely, he teaches that the conscious labour and intentional suffering of the individual produces results far beyond his own personal experience. The words, "Seek ye first the kingdom of God and His righteousness, and all these things shall be added unto you," apply not only to food and clothing but also to all the things which are essentially necessary for the ordinary natural life of man. By working on himself man becomes a free being with the power of self-judgment and also with the power of impartial criticism of any situation with which he is confronted. With liberation from his own egoism he is also liberated from suggestibility and dependence upon the opinions of others. Thus alone can he become capable of being a citizen of a world upon which great forces play. I have already referred to Gurdjieff's explanation of war as the result of two independent factors, the first of which is the periodic arising of states of tension which manifest themselves in the inward experience of people as dissatisfaction and unrest. If this disturbance takes the form of a dissatisfaction with one's own being and a greater urge to hasten forward with the work of self-perfection, it can produce at an accelerated tempo a widespread improvement in the whole human situation. If, however, dissatisfaction is outwardly directed towards external conditions of life and towards other people, it can lead only to war and revolution—the processes of mutual destruction which are the greatest shame of the human race.

It is the tragedy of contemporary religion in every part of the world that these fundamental truths, clearly stated by the Sacred Individuals, are so completely disregarded that religion itself has for the time being ceased to be an effective power in the life of man.

CHAPTER V

THE AIMLESSNESS OF OUR EXISTENCE

IN the course of the previous chapters I have had occasion to discuss various aims for the attainment of which a human being might be expected to exercise that power of choice which is his birthright. The first is the aim *to be*. It is for Gurdjieff a fundamental proposition that man is not man until he makes himself so. He is a thinking animal with the possibility of becoming a man. He is a slave with just sufficient power of choice to enable him, if he exercises it, to attain real freedom. He should be a free independent individual. If he sees the contrast between what he is and what he might be, he can begin to experience a hunger for being and from this derive at least one stable permanent aim. For contemporary men and women, almost without exception, such an aim does not exist and its possibility is not even suspected. Man lives as he is, and dies as he is, with vague fears and vague hopes but no clarity of purpose and no experience of need for self-creation in the sense of being.

Whereas the aim to create one's own being may appear self-centred and therefore not wholly worthy of occupying a dominating position in our lives, this cannot be said of the obligation to prepare the coming generation for a becoming human existence. I have tried to show that, although in most parents and teachers the desire to fulfil this obligation may be present, the understanding of what is involved and the power to do it are completely lacking. All those things which are most essential for a becoming adult life are either neglected or pursued with ignorance and misunderstanding such as to produce results quite opposite to what is hoped for. The general helplessness in the task of preparing children for adult life is lost sight of in the ever-growing complexity of educational systems, directed, it is true, almost exclusively to the teaching of things which are useless for practical life but which nevertheless disguise from people the extent of their failure. It is only when obvious disasters occur that parents are seized with remorse at the harm they have done their children. Far more often the harm passes unnoticed and the parents pride themselves upon the sacrifices they have made to give their children a "good education."

The attainment of valid knowledge about man, the universe and the relations between man and the universe is a legitimate and indeed, a noble, aim, and it has been zealously pursued by some people at most periods. This aim of true objective science has been virtually entirely lost in modern times through our preoccupation with the study of isolated details and our tendency to assess results in terms of accidental achievements in the field of technology. Man has almost entirely lost interest in those departments of knowledge which are decisive for his welfare—that is, knowledge of what he is, what purpose he was created to serve, and of the means he should employ to enable him to fulfil his destiny. The aim to answer the question given in the title of this book, "What are we living for?" may arise from time to time in a desultory fashion in many people's minds; but for how very few is it a burning question which must be answered.

There are some who would say that the question is not one to be answered by the way of knowledge but by the way of faith; that the answer to the question is already given in religion: to serve God and to do his will. It is worship and sanctification through worship. It is asserted by many people that it is precisely the absence of any such aim among the great majority of peoples that is responsible for the dangerous situation into which mankind has drifted. I tried to show in the previous chapter that the responsibility for this lies to no small extent with those who have distorted and diluted with their own imaginings the demand clearly expressed in the recorded teachings of the great religious Founders. Nominal religion or half-hearted religion is no religion at all.

Leaving aside aims of a general character, we can think also of specific purposes which people might be expected to serve with a whole-hearted and non-egoistic desire; such an aim is the abolition of war, and there are indeed many people today who with ardour and devotion address themselves singly or through various societies to the accomplishment of this task.

That such a process, so abhorrent to any thinking

person and so immediately disastrous to the very people who become involved in it, should continue unchecked is a mystery which cannot be explained in ordinary terms. Our inability, just as manifest today as at any period in human history, to prevent armed conflict—whether in war, civil war or revolution—must be regarded as a most convincing demonstration of our ignorance of the forces which operate to determine the destiny of mankind. If only one person in every ten throughout the countries which have in our lifetime experienced the horror of war, were to devote to the task of preventing war the energy which the remaining nine devote to self-indulgence, the whole history of mankind would be changed. If those who are doomed to perish miserably in the next war could but see the future and realize that by their efforts war could be prevented, perhaps they would feel the urge to do the necessary work. But no one sees reality and the aim to prevent war remains the pastime of a handful of cranks and enthusiasts.

If all these great aims play so small a part in human life, what are in fact the dominant motives of the average man or woman? First of all, the greater part of the day is occupied with the simple needs of the animal body, eating and sleeping and the labour necessary to provide for food, clothing and shelter. In so far as this part of their lives is concerned, men and women do not differ from animals unless they import some additional value in terms of inner experience or the development of their being which an animal cannot have. Animals seek food and eat it; they reproduce their kind and care for their young; they rest their bodies in sleep and perform the totality of those functions which are required to serve the general trans- formation of substance which, according to Gurdjieff's teaching, is the purpose of the second fundamental mode of being. Man likewise eats and is eaten, and in doing so serves precisely the same general purpose as every other animal. He cannot escape from this purpose and there is, on the whole, little significant difference in the proportion of the total time and energy which he devotes to it whether he is a so-called primitive savage or a civilized man, whether he is an Asiatic, a European or an American.

There are two ways in which man can draw a distinc- tion between himself and a mere animal. The first is the manner in which he performs his necessary animal functions, and the second is the use he makes of the time and energy at his disposal beyond that required by his animal needs. Let us begin by comparing the performance of the essentially animal functions. These may proceed in solitude, but do so more usually in the environment of family life. How does the human family compare with the animal family? That it has possibilities far transcending that of animal existence no one can deny. But how far are these possibilities realized? Almost without exception there is in the family life of animals, whether among those perma- nently mated or those whose unity is determined by the season only, a harmony and a singleness of purpose which, though limited, are nevertheless nearly complete. Without sparing themselves, animals and birds devote virtually the whole of their energies during the mating season to the heavy task of producing and preparing the next generation. Such bickering and such quarrels, such gentleness and such harshness as can be observed, obviously serve some biological purpose. In human families, especially among "civilized" peoples, many unseemly features which are absent or almost absent from animal life, tend to destroy the harmony and frustrate the purpose of family life. Jealousy, envy, partiality, suspicion, possessiveness, the desire for power, laziness, the shirking of responsibility, and all the other manifestations of egoism enter in varying degrees into all human relationships—not excepting those of blood. Of all that we most admire in the lives of families, such as disinterested self- sacrifice even to the point of death, do we not find these also among animals, birds and even fishes?

> "The wren, the most diminutive of birds, will fight,
> Her young ones in her nest, against the owl."

All these things have been said so often and so well that they have brought into play that characteristic power of man by which he can cease to feel, or even to see, what is not comforting to his self-esteem. It is sufficient that we should establish the point that, except insofar as the human family is united by some higher purpose than to serve mere animal existence,

it cannot claim a value higher than that of other
animals.

If we turn our attention to the process whereby
the necessities of life, food, clothing and shelter are
secured, we must differentiate between its performance
as a mere necessity and its use as a medium of self-
expression and a means of self-creation. It is here that
the modern world stands wretchedly condemned. For
the overwhelming majority of people, both men and
women, their daily labour is neither the one nor the
other. It is performed either grudgingly or mechani-
cally under the compulsion of need and automatized
habit. For the comparatively few who are not driven
by compulsion, the motives for labour are usually
even less worthy of praise. Personal ambition, the
desire for power or for the means of gratifying various
appetites, play a very great part. Even where these are
not obviously present, there is especially in modern
times—a tendency to prize occupation for its own sake,
as a means of stifling thought and stifling particularly
the question which arises from something very deep
and very real in almost every human being: "For what
am I living and what purpose does my existence really
serve?" In these things our human capacity for self-deception is wonderfully displayed. Men and women of
great ability, with great understanding of the purpose
for which they should use their powers, can succeed in
convincing themselves that in building up great organizations, in multiplying the means of producing material

wealth, in planning and directing the lives of thousands or millions of other human beings, they are doing something which is worthy. If it is demonstrated to them that all their activity does nothing to diminish the sum of human sufferings, to prevent the disaster of war or, more specifically, to raise human life to a higher level of experience and understanding, they either become indignant or helplessly protest that there is nothing better for them to do. In the meantime, the general mechanization of human labour proceeds apace. Joy disappears from daily work, with the inevitable accompaniment of a growing apathy and indifference which no one who travels through the industrial countries of the world can fail to perceive with apprehension and dismay. Except in a few small communities whose lives should serve as a reminder to the rest of the world of the precious thing which has ''been lost, labour as an act of worship is a forgotten or derided conception.

Finally, we come to the enjoyment (so-called) of leisure (so-called). Here, if anywhere, we could expect to find the real meaning which should attach to the proud name of Man. Having performed the functions imposed upon us by our animal nature we are free to manifest the glory of our human nature. I can scarcely find it in my heart to write further, for the reader must be as painfully aware as I am of the pitiful tale to be told. At the very least, leisure should be the opportunity for creative self-expression. It should, in fact, be far more: it should be the means of undertaking the noblest work to which a man can set his hand—the creation of his own being and the payment of the debt which he owes to the Universe so that he may ultimately be fitted to fulfil the hopes of his Creator as an active participant in the realization of the Divine Purpose.

What does he do? He leaves his work to return home, often to quarrel with his family, sometimes to spoil his children by indulgence or perhaps to spend the evening in a half-conscious passive condition, listening to the wireless or drinking and gossiping in the public house. If he goes out of doors at all, it is on Saturdays to sit equally passively watching a football match or to experience the excitement of gambling at the races. His wife has in any case so little leisure that it is scarcely fair to ask her how she spends it. Or, if we are thinking of those who have more money and more leisure, we see them for the most part either drinking senselessly, without enjoyment, or indulging in promiscuous sexual adventures with scarcely more decency than the ancient Romans used. At best, they talk of things they do not understand—discuss the play they have seen (which is in any case not worth discussing); the book they have read (which was in any case not worth reading). And all are united, irrespective of class, by that great modern invention for "killing" time, the cinema.

Against all this miserable passivity there are, of course, reactions. Some take opportunities for study; others work in various organizations devoted to some good cause. But it is in these very reactions that the tragedy of the whole situation becomes apparent—for even those who are satisfied that the meaningless-ness of their existence can find nothing to do which is truly creative either of their own being or of a better situation in the life of man. The very excellence of their intentions, the very ardour with which these would-be beneficial purposes are pursued, serve only to show that there is indeed something in man which aspires to serve a greater purpose than that of animal existence, and to demonstrate that we have lost the understanding of how this is to be done.

CHAPTER VI

WHAT SHALL IT PROFIT A MAN?

IT is recorded in St. Mark's Gospel that when Jesus had called together the people and his disciples, he taught them explicitly that in order to live it is necessary to die and that whoever was unwilling to die could not hope to live. And then he asked the question which still stands as the supreme challenge to mankind: "For what shall it profit a man, if he shall gain the whole world, and lose his own soul? Or what shall a man give in exchange for his soul?"

Such sayings as these have little more weight than that of any other moral exhortation for those who deny, or even doubt, that he who uttered them was a Sacred Individual sent from God with the task of reopening the way of salvation for mankind. They are free to interpret them as they will, but those who profess to believe that Jesus was a divinely inspired Teacher are under an obligation to take seriously and to search for the meaning of a statement made in such clear, unequivocal terms. Disastrous mistakes must inevitably follow from any refusal to take such statements literally, simply because they do not readily fit into some preconceived theory as to the nature of the reality to which they refer.

In this passage the words *gain* and *loss* are placed in

antithesis to one another, with precise and unequivocal reference to the soul. The soul is thus something which can be gained or lost. It is not an inalienable possession but something for which a price *(ἀντάλλαγμα)* has to be paid; with the implication, "No payment, no soul."

Now this conception of the soul runs counter to that which had become almost universal in Greek thought at the time when that same Greek thought began to provide material for the elaboration of a Christian theology. The Greek doctrine of the immortal soul was adopted, notwithstanding the clear evidence in the most authentic *logia* of Jesus that this was contrary to his own weighty teaching. From this truly unpardonable distortion there arose doctrines of the soul which conceived it as in any case assured in all circumstances of an everlasting existence, and in consequence subject to eternal reward or punishment according to whether or not the quality of the actions performed during life reached or failed to reach a certain standard of merit. The absurdity of this doctrine when carried to its logical conclusion—namely, that every soul must fall in one of the two categories of the eternally saved and the eternally damned, has been one of the major causes of the decay of Christian faith; It is due entirely to the failure of the early systematizers of Christian teaching—bemused by the prestige of Greek philosophy—to see the meaning of what was plainly written in passages which they could not but take to be an authentic record of the sayings of the Founder.

For Jesus, the soul was something to be gained or lost; and to gain a soul it was necessary to pay the price, namely, the relegating of all other values to an inferior status. I have already referred to the five times repeated passage: "To him that hath shall be given; and from him that hath not, shall be taken away even that which he hath." I cannot doubt that this means, "to him that hath paid the price and thereby gained a soul shall be given eternal life. From him that hath lost his soul shall be taken away even that temporal life which he hath."

I have approached the discussion of human destiny in this manner because in speaking and lecturing upon the subject I have almost invariably encountered a violent objection to the notion that man has to create his own soul by his own labour, and until he has done so he has no soul at all. I always find it strange to listen to the vehemence with which people insist that they must have a soul that is born with them and cannot die. If, indeed, they had a soul with such attributes it would be a possession so precious that its care should be their first concern. But the very people who insist that they have a soul have usually spent their lives in complete disregard of its needs and the means whereby its eternal welfare can be assured. There is seldom very much difference in the behaviour of those who profess to believe in the existence of the soul and those who deny it as an outworn superstition. The sceptical request: "Produce your soul and show me what it is," is unanswerable for the man who has nothing in him that is permanent and reliable, who cannot control his own actions, who is riddled with inner contradictions and who, moreover, cannot indicate any single process in. either his inward experience or his external behaviour which cannot be fully explained in terms of his physical body and its functions.

Retribution for great mistakes can be very terrible, especially where a fundamentally unworthy motive underlies what may appear to be an honest failure to understand. Belief that every man, automatically and without efforts on his own part, is the possessor of an immortal soul arose together with the Megalanthropic fallacy about which I wrote in *The Crisis in Human Affairs*. The impulse to believe in the infinite value of the human individual led naturally to the ascription of an attribute which appeared to lift him above the plane of ordinary mortal existence. So it came about that at an early stage of the development of Christian thought the doctrine of the immortal soul and the doctrine of the infinite value of the human individual arose together. Neither is justified by the facts disclosed in all human experience, nor does either find any sanction in the teaching of the Founder of Christianity. I have confined myself in this discussion to Christian teaching, but it is worth remembering that denial of the existence in man of a soul was from the start an integral part of the teaching of Gotama Buddha.

Gurdjieff's teaching in regard to the soul is clear and explicit. According to him, the soul is the consequence of the actions performed during life. If a man's actions have no purpose and therefore no pattern, if they are riddled with inconsistency and contradiction and therefore annul one another, and if they consist exclusively or almost exclusively of mere animal automatisms, no soul is produced. Such a man lives as an animal and like an animal he perishes and is destroyed forever. In so far as a man conceives and sets before himself an aim and struggles consistently for the attainment of that aim, the results of his actions crystallize in such a way as to produce something independent of his physical body. This "something" is his soul, and its degree of completeness and perfection depends upon the quality of his aim and the intensity of the efforts which he has made in order to achieve it.

In using the words "completeness" and "perfection", I have left unexpressed a distinction which plays a large part in Gurdjieff's ideas. This is the division of the soul into two parts, successively acquired, and corresponding to two very different stages of inner development.

The tradition that man is, or rather should be, composed of three parts is very ancient. It is expressed in the words, "body, soul and spirit," although these words have been given meanings which are very far from the reality. St. Paul scarcely uses the word 'soul' except in the colloquial sense to mean a person, as in the passage, "let every soul be subject to the higher powers." He refers instead to different bodies, particularly to the body of the Resurrection.

He makes use of the terms, carnal, natural, spiritual, and asserts that the natural is prior to the spiritual. He certainly does not conceive the spiritual body—that is, the body of the Resurrection—as something naturally and inevitably present in man but rather as the reward of steadfast faith and the works of righteousness. It is reserved exclusively for the few who are to participate in the Resurrection.

I have referred to the Christian tradition because it is scarcely necessary to discuss the Eastern doctrines of higher bodies conceived as vehicles for the higher functions of man. Owing always to the uncritical acceptance of the Greek notion of the soul as indestructible (a notion, by the way, about which most Greek philosophers themselves had considerable misgivings), western interpreters of Eastern literature have often taken for granted, entirely without justification, that the higher bodies spoken of exist naturally in a man in much the same way as his physical body exists, except that they are made of finer matters which render them in varying degrees exempt from that decay and dissolution which, for the physical body, is the inevitable end. All such ideas are misleading and dangerous; for they conduce to a process of self-deception by giving colour to the comforting thought that if one already has something immortal, one need only avoid doing it some grievous injury and all will be well.

With the care for precise and unequivocal statement that characterizes the recorded parables of Jesus, we find the whole situation made clear in the parable of the man without a wedding garment. The wedding garment is something which the man did not possess by nature, which he should have taken pains to prepare for himself and without which it is impossible for him, even if he were invited, to participate in the wedding feast. The highest body of man, his immortal soul, is not something which he possesses by nature; it is something which he has to create for himself by his own conscious labour and intentional suffering and without which he cannot participate in the purposes for which he was destined by his Creator. I began this chapter with a discussion of the soul because this seemed to be the simplest way of expressing what Gurdjieff means by speaking of man as a self-creating being. In order to make his position a little more understandable I must now speak about two further important elements of his teaching. The first concerns the nature of man and the reason why he is able to do what an animal cannot. The second is to answer the question inevitably posed: Why is it, if such wonderful things are possible for man, that so few attain them and so many cannot even be brought to see that they exist?

In the chapter on Education, I stated that Gurdjieff conceives man as a three-brained being capable of three independent modes of experience—thinking, feeling and sensing. Animals are two-brained or one-brained beings; that is, they can sense or they can both feel and sense, but they cannot perform the three functions of sensing, feeling and thinking that are possible for man. Although it is through his thinking part that man acquires a possibility denied to animals, his sensing and feeling parts are equally essential to the process of self-creation. If a man withdraws his experience from his feeling and sensing parts, and identifies his own existence with that in him which thinks, he not only becomes unbalanced but he also loses touch with processes which, although he is unaware of them, nevertheless exercise a decisive influence upon the whole of his behaviour. Man can thus be said to have three personalities: with one of these he feels, with one he thinks, and with the third he senses. Instead of treating the two subconscious personalities merely as sources of disturbances in the working of the thinking brain, Gurdjieff teaches that they must be developed and brought into consciousness, that they contain certain powers and can perform certain functions of which the thinking brain itself is not capable. In particular, he ascribes to the feeling brain the all-important function of conscience—that is, the power of impartial self-judgment. The thinking brain inevitably makes its judgments in terms of preexisting associations and by comparison with standards abstractly conceived. This leads to the false notion of an external good and evil, capable of expression in terms of formulae and rules. The only ultimately reliable guide is that conscience which, in the average man—mainly owing to defective education—is buried deep in the subconscious processes of his feeling brain.

It is a reliable guide for the very reason that it springs from a source deeper than man himself: it is called by Gurdjieff in one of his writings, the REPRESENTATIVE OF THE CREATOR. The only experience of conscience known to the average man is remorse, an experience which should drive him to genuine "being" efforts. One of the principal objectives of man's work upon himself is to awaken his conscience and thus gain the capacity for impartial objective judgment.

The work undertaken with the aim of self-creation does not produce its results only in the inner life of man, but also, and eminently, in the transformation of human relations. Those who have understood the necessity for this work recognise and respect in other people the presence of a like understanding. The mutual appraisement of people is transferred from external and frequently accidental manifestations to the assessment of the clarity and strength of the inner desire *to become that which one ought to be.*

This conception is illustrated with particular force and vividness in Gurdjieff's attitude towards the causes of war and the means of its prevention. I wrote in the first chapter that he regards war as the consequence of two independent factors, the first of which is the periodic arising of a state of tension in which a feeling of dissatisfaction with their own slavery takes possession of people. Now two completely opposite reactions to this feeling are possible. In a man who understands that the causes of his own slavery reside in his own lack of being, the effect is to stimulate him to greater and more persistent efforts towards self-perfection. The tempo of this work is accelerated and at such periods important changes for the future of the world become possible. This can occur, however, only if the realization is sufficiently widespread and a sufficiently large proportion of people respond to the feeling of dissatisfaction in this positive way. If, on the contrary, the causes of dissatisfaction are conceived as external, people translate the experience into an impulse of fear or anger. Tension and misunderstanding grow and the impulse to destruction presents itself as a need for defense against some threatened danger or to gain a freedom wrongly withheld by others. Revolution and civil war, or war between nations, then becomes inevitable. The same process is manifested in individuals by an increase in insanity, in the number of suicides and divorces and in the spread of unnatural vices.

Various questions, which really are one question, arise when the human situation is presented in such a light. First of all, we must ask why it is, if the process of self-creation is so straightforward and if its fruits are precious above all that belongs to ordinary life, that people have neither recognized it, nor been able to accept it and live accordingly even when they have been shown the way. Or we may ask, if the causes of war really lie in the failure of people to respond to feelings of dissatisfaction by increase in efforts, why do these causes on the contrary appear to us as outward manifestations of ill-intentioned people seeking power for their own selfish, ends? Or, and above all, why is it that whereas people can make great and persistent efforts for the attainment of some visible objective they are quite unable to make corresponding efforts for their own welfare and that of their fellow-men? Why does the question: "What shall it profit a man, if he gain the whole world, and lose his own soul?" leave the vast majority of people unmoved and unresponsive?

The answer which Gurdjieff gives to this last question is so fundamental that it can be understood only by careful and persistent study of his writings. In one sense it is a reconstruction of the doctrine of original sin, but it is also a restatement which removes from this doctrine the objections which have hitherto made it so difficult to understand and accept. Man suffers from a tendency to self-deception and illusion for which he cannot be blamed except in so far as he fails to struggle against it. It is hereditary; it has been transmitted to him from his remote ancestors. It goes back, in fact, to the great transformation in human nature which took place at the period of the emergence of our modern races from primitive man, who existed previous to the last great Ice Age. These primitive races, of whom the Neanderthal man can be taken as the type, were three-brained beings and as such were different in their essential nature from animals with two or only one brain. They were able to maintain their existence and survive the terrible changes of climate and other dangers of the early world because their thinking brain gave them a power of adaptation which no animal possessed. According to Gurdjieff's cosmological conceptions there were specific reasons connected with the economy of the solar system, and in particular with the relations between the earth and the moon, which made it necessary that for a very long period of time the human brain should be used only for the purposes of what effectively was an animal existence. At a definite moment of time this necessity ceased to operate, and thereafter it became possible for man to assume his proper place in the cosmic economy as a self-creating being able to liberate himself from his own animal nature. The transformation took place, not by a process of blind adaptation—200,000 years of static existence suggests that this was impossible—but by a conscious intervention from a higher level. This Gurdjieff represents as a process whereby a certain organ, present in the remote ancestors of mankind, was removed, and man was restored to the power of choice, and the ability to understand his own nature and his real destiny. With the removal of this organ there emerged the precursors of our modern races, whose skeleton remains show them to have been developed in their physical characteristics—and above all in their cranial capacity—to a level fully equal to that of contemporary man. Prehistoric research tends to show that the transformation took place during the course of a few thousand years—an extremely short space of time compared with the immense period of stationary existence by which it was preceded. There appeared in the world with startling suddenness tall fair races, short brown races, negroid races, all with large brains and some with powers and skills which arouse wonder as their achievements come to light. Palaeolithic art as exemplified in the cave paintings—particularly those of Altamira and Lascaux—has qualities of realism and deep feeling which have scarcely been equaled by any succeeding period. These men must also have accomplished the miracles of the domestication of animals and the creation of language. They laid the foundations of the modern world.

Had the transformation from *Homo neanderthalensis* to *Homo sapiens* been as complete inwardly as it was in its outward manifestations, the whole subsequent history of the world would have been different. According to the researches of Gurdjieff, which are embodied in his system, the transformation was defective in one vital respect: the organ which prevented primitive man from being any more than a thinking animal was, indeed, removed, but the behaviour pattern developed by countless generations while it was operative had become a hereditary taint from which the newly liberated races could have freed themselves only by a conscious effort. The effort was not made, or at least it was not made successfully. In consequence, subsequent generations remained subject to a tendency to attach undue importance to their animal life and disregard the new inheritance into which they had entered. No longer a thinking animal by necessity, man began to develop a mechanism of self-justification whereby he could use his new-found powers for unworthy purposes without experiencing remorse of conscience. Thus began, and ever since has continued, a disastrous situation in which mankind has failed to fulfil the hopes for which it was created. "For this people's heart is waxed gross, and their ears are dull of hearing, and their eyes they have closed lest at any time they should see with their eyes and hear with their ears, and should understand with their heart, and should be converted, and I should heal them."

Left to its own devices in this unfortunate situation, mankind would inevitably have relapsed into its previous state of savagery and all possibility of fulfilling its destiny would have disappeared. By the will of the All-Just and All-Merciful Creator, Sacred Individuals have successively been incarnated in human form for the purpose of showing mankind, if possible, a way of salvation. This has happened not once but many times, and each time a different fundamental conception has served as the basis of their teaching. According to an ancient tradition, which Gurdjieff approves, there was one period in which the task was very nearly successfully accomplished, when for a certain time the greater part of the world lived with the understanding that man must seek his own conscience and strive to live by it. This was the legendary Golden Age, of which no record remains save vague rumours significant only for their ubiquity in all the traditions of all the races of mankind. The Sacred individuals are represented as moved by an infinite compassion towards the sufferings of mankind, but by the very fact of their incarnation in human form they themselves were not exempt from the possibility of error. Nevertheless, by their labours alone has the possibility been kept open for a return of mankind to its highest destiny as the source of self-perfected individuals able in their turn to serve the purposes of their Creator.

The whole of Gurdjieff's teaching on this subject is so important and so significant that to my mind it provides an indispensable element without which no convincing interpretation of the human situation is possible.

In conclusion, I should perhaps make a brief reference to the conception of eternity at which I myself arrived from essentially physical considerations. It is based in the first instance upon an examination of the character of the temporal process and the apparent universal validity of the two, as they are termed, laws of thermodynamics. The observation that everything that exists in time is subject to the requirement that there should be a permanent, exact regulation of the quantity of mass energy present in the universe, and approximately, also, that present in any virtually closed system, must lead to the acceptance of a mechanistic determinism from which the possibility of free choice is banished. The further observation, also inescapable, that everything that exists in time is subject to a process of inevitable dissolution and ultimate disintegration, which—though theoretically reversible, is only so to a vanishingly small degree of probability—colours the mechanistic picture with an added tinge of hopelessness. Not only is everything that happens bound to happen, but it is also bound to happen in such a way that the differentiations from which alone any significance could be attached to its existence, must ultimately, disappear. I can see no escape from this conclusion except to postulate an ampler reality in which the necessary degree of freedom can be recovered. Such a reality can be found simply, and I think adequately, in the conception of eternity as a fifth dimension in which the operation of the laws of thermodynamics is reversed.* This permits us to conceive different levels of which only the last is completely determined and entirely subject to the observed thermodynamic laws. It is this level alone which is disclosed by our sense perceptions which provide the whole of the data for natural science. It is in our conscious experience that we can liberate ourselves from the deterministic process; but this implies an act of creation for the gaps in the causal sequence necessary for freedom can be filled only by making something which is not there. Carried to the logical conclusion, this line of thought leads us to conceive a level in eternity from which causality has disappeared entirely and is replaced by a situation in which free creative activity is the only law.

* A mathematical treatment of this theory is given in "Unified Field Theory in a Curvature Free Five-Dimensional Manifold." J.G. Bennett, R.L. Brown and M.W. Thring. *Proc. Roy. Soc.*, July 1949.

Gurdjieff does not introduce the word, Eternity, into his exposition in the precise sense in which I have used it; but his doctrine of levels of being fully corresponds to that which can be formulated in terms of the interpenetration of time and eternity. He frequently uses the term "Above", and makes it clear that this implies a realm of being in which freedom reaches the highest possible degree within the limits of the created world. The Beings who can exist on this level are Sacred Individuals whose task it is to perform the highest of all possible functions—the redemption of the universe from the otherwise inevitable consequences of its existence in time. At the summit he places the Creator, infinitely just and infinitely loving, but nevertheless bound by the necessities of his own inscrutable purpose to permit the inviolate operation of those laws which determine the very existence of the universe he has made.

With the aid of these conceptions we can answer the question: "What are we living for?" in terms which can satisfy our minds no less than our feelings. There is a cosmic purpose which can be served only by free beings. In each one of us the seed of free individuality is planted from Above. The choice before us is slavery to that which is below or service to that which is above. Slavery is misery and acceptance of slavery means ultimate and final destruction. Freedom is not only the greatest happiness, but it is also the only state in which we can serve our fellow-men and fulfil the purpose for which we are created.

But the price of freedom is conscious labour and intentional suffering, that is, the unrelenting struggle with our own defects and weakness and the sacrifice of all lesser aims. If we set ourselves the aim of achieving Free Individuality we must not forget the words of the Upanishad: "Not by description may that Self be found, nor by thought, nor by much learning. To him who makes it his sole and only aim, to him alone that Self reveals its own true nature. He who has not ceased from wrong action, who is not inwardly peaceful, who is not prepared and whose mind is not tranquil, cannot gain knowledge of that Self. Wise teaching alone and well directed effort can lead to its attainment. If taught by an inferior man, it cannot be understood in spite of mental effort. Save by right teaching there is no way to it, for its subtlety transcends the subtlety of thought."

It is useless to set before man lofty aims and great purposes which are utterly beyond his present powers, without at the same time showing him the way to gain the understanding and the strength which he lacks. The supreme merits of Gurdjieff's teaching are, on the one hand, the full weight which it gives to human infirmity, and on the other, the clear and practical guidance it offers at every stage of the way towards that change of human nature the necessity for which I have sought to establish.

WHO IS GURDJIEFF?

TO those who take an interest in such things it has been known for many years that a remarkable teacher had come to the West in the person of a man reputed to have gained access to sources of knowledge denied to any previous western explorer. Since nothing authentic and, indeed, very little of any kind has ever been published about Gurdjieff's teaching, he and his work have given rise to many rumours and to much misunderstanding. To these rumours and to this misunderstanding he has paid no regard at all; he has continued to work with a small group of permanent followers and a somewhat larger circle of students intermittently in personal contact with him to prepare for what he at all times has declared to be his ultimate intention: the publication of his discoveries for the benefit of the world. He has recently decided that the time has come when this decisive step could be undertaken, and those of us who have had the good fortune to benefit from his personal teaching have the responsibility of ensuring, as far as this is possible, that the importance which we have come to attach to them be shared by those to whom they soon will be addressed.

Gurdjieff has passed his eighty-third birthday.

That he is a man of great knowledge and even greater powers cannot be doubted by anyone who has come in personal contact with him. His unwearying readiness to succour the physical no less than the spiritual needs of those who go to him for help, is a sufficient attestation of his love towards his fellow-men. His fortitude in the most extreme physical suffering and his indifference to external conditions of life—often in every respect painful—are indications of an inner strength which indeed can be felt in everything that he does. More than this I need not say at the present time.

Of his searches and the means whereby he arrived at his undoubted great knowledge, not only of the latent possibilities in man but of the means and methods whereby they can be developed, little has been made public. He was born in the Caucasus, of an old Greek family which migrated more than a hundred years ago from one of the ancient Greek colonies of Asia Minor. From his early childhood he had opportunities of meeting with a series of remarkable men, from contact with whom he acquired the conviction that something of vital importance was missing from the views about man and the world current in the European science and literature he had been set to study. He was educated with the intention that he might either become a physician or a priest; but his dissatisfaction with the limitations of his education, both medical and theological, drove him to seek for himself.

With a group of people mostly much older than

himself he travelled for many years in many parts
of Africa, Asia and the Far East, ultimately reaching
places the very existence of which is unsuspected by
more orthodox explorers. Of where he went and what
he found, it would be inappropriate for me to say
anything. He has declared his intention of making these
things known in the second series of his writings; these
will become available only after the publication of the
first series the scope of which is indicated by their title,
An Objectively Impartial Criticism of the Life of Man.

The first phase of Gurdjieff's life-work was completed
in the early years of the present century, when he had
found and decided how to use the knowledge which he
was seeking. The second phase is a period of more than
forty years during which he has been experimenting and
testing the methods by which this knowledge can best
be transmitted in a form suitable for the requirements
of the modern world. I myself first met him in 1921 in
Constantinople, to which he had come from the Caucasus
with a small group of his immediate disciples. He there
demonstrated, among other things, his methods of work
through the use of gymnastic exercises, occupational
rhythms and sacred dances which, from time immemo-
rial, had been employed in certain Asiatic countries to
assist the harmonious development of powers latent in
man. My first contact with him and his ideas convinced
me that I was in the presence of a new and living force.

In 1922 he founded near Paris his Institute for the

Harmonious Development of Man, at the Château du Prieuré at Fontainebleau. Many people, mostly English, visited this Institute for shorter or longer periods during the years 1923 and 1924. In 1924 he went to America to organize a branch of the Institute there and to give demonstrations of the movements which formed an important part of his method of work. On his return from America a terrible motor accident, from the results of which I believe any ordinary man would have died, obliged him to discontinue the work of the Institute and, for various reasons, he decided to abandon the plan of transmitting his ideas through personal teaching and demonstrations on a large scales and devote himself instead to embodying them in a series of writings; these occupied him to the virtual exclusion of all other activities until 1930. From 1930 until the outbreak of the last war he was engaged partly in writing and partly in teaching small groups of disciples in France and the United States. Throughout the last war he was in Paris, where he continued his work under conditions of great personal difficulty. It was not until 1948 that he judged the time was ripe for a resumption of his larger plans, and he then began to collect round him again not only his immediate disciples but also those followers of his ideas who, like myself, had been struggling to understand and apply his teaching without the advantage of his own personal guidance.

With this step was ushered in the third phase of Gurdjieff's life-work: the realization of his original intention to make his ideas available to the world at large.

This brief account of Gurdjieff's teaching and his work would not be complete if I did not make some reference to the extraordinary rumours with which he has been surrounded. He is a man who is entirely indifferent to the friendly or hostile opinion of other people towards him. Not only this, but for reasons very often incomprehensible at the time even to those closely in contact with him, he has apparently gone out of his way to arouse antagonisms and cause misunderstandings. It has often happened that only very much later have the reasons which required that such action be taken, become apparent. To those who understand that his teaching contains something which is indispensable for their own welfare, and without which they cannot hope to attain the aim of their existence, the difficulties which he places in the way of approach represent a small price which is easily paid. To those who find them a formidable deterrent I can only say that every great teaching, in its inception, has appeared at once as a stumbling-block and a foolishness.

All this applies to the first series of Gurdjieff's writings, to be published under the title of *An Objectively Impartial Criticism of the Life of Man*, or, *Beelzebub's Tales to his Grandson*. For those who have studied these writings assiduously, without preconception or prejudice, they contain the means of acquiring a point of view which is indispensable for a right understanding of the human situation. They also contain—though in a form which it requires persistence and determination to piece together—a system of thought which, for the majesty of its conception and the concrete practical character of its application, is of an entirely different order from the speculations, theories and dogmas with which mankind is seeking to live today.

Made in the USA
Las Vegas, NV
29 May 2022

49504089R00104